UNDERSTANDING THE BOOKS OF THE NEW TESTAMENT

UNDERSTANDING
THE BOOKS OF THE
NEW TESTAMENT

A GUIDE TO BIBLE STUDY FOR LAYMEN

Edited by

PATRICK H. CARMICHAEL

Prepared by

FELIX B. GEAR   ·   PAUL LESLIE GARBER

JOSEPH M. GARRISON   ·   HENRY WADE DUBOSE

PATRICK D. MILLER   ·   JAMES E. BEAR

JOHN KNOX PRESS   ATLANTA

Fifth printing 1976
International Standard Book Number: ISBN-0-8042-3304-7
Library of Congress Catalog Card Number: 61:9583

All Scripture quotations are from the American Standard Version (1901).

PREFACE TO THE REVISED EDITION

The editor of the John Knox Press has given me the privilege of preparing such revisions of this volume as may seem to be indicated by a careful reading of the material. I am proposing a few changes which I think will be helpful in the realization of the purpose set forth originally for the publication of such a work.

The principle changes occur in the section devoted to the General Epistles where it is believed that the reader will be greatly helped by breaking the material up into divisions in such a way that he can see at a glance the chief emphases. This should be helpful as he progresses in his reading and for purposes of review. The original content has not been materially changed.

A careful rereading of this material has given me a new appreciation of the original concept which guided the preparation of the manuscript, and for the splendid content which has been written into it by the several authors. So far as I know this is the only volume which offers the lay reader so much valuable guidance material for the self-study of the New Testament. It is a resource which when used with the Bible, the Bible dictionary, and the commentary provides the earnest student unlimited assistance in his search for an understanding of the teachings of the Scriptures.

As this volume goes into its third printing, with revisions as indicated above, it is the sincere hope of the Editor that it will receive continued favor by students of the Bible and that its usefulness will be increased through the years.

Patrick H. Carmichael
Princeton, New Jersey

PREFACE

In the preface to *Understanding the Books of the Old Testament* the editor expressed the conviction that there should be a guide to Bible study written particularly for the lay man and woman. The necessity for a second printing in slightly more than a year after its appearance from the press is reassuring evidence for the justification of such a conviction and for the publication of the companion volume on the New Testament.*

We are presenting in this volume a series of six brief studies, each a complete unit in itself, which are so related as collectively to make a complete survey of the New Testament. The writers were requested to limit their manuscripts to a maximum of ten thousand words. Obviously such a brief work cannot contain sufficient material to provide all the guidance in study that is needed. The writers were requested, therefore, to confine their references largely to three resource volumes: the *American Standard Version of the Bible, The Westminster Dictionary of the Bible* by Davis and Gehman, and *The One Volume Bible Commentary* by Dummelow.† We recognize many other good dictionaries and commentaries which should be used freely by those who have access to them. Our purpose was to so limit reference material that individuals and groups might secure adequate resources in a comparatively small number of volumes and be assured of helps at hand for a long and continuous study of the Scriptures. Quotations from the American Standard Version are used by permission of the National Council of the Churches of Christ in the United States of America.

We have endeavored to provide a comprehensive and constructive guide to individual study, for use in Bible classes in the Sunday school and elsewhere, as a basis for several courses in the Standard Leadership curriculum, as a rapid survey course for students in

---

* The fifth printing of the Old Testament volume was made in 1958 and a revised edition in 1961.

† Readers of the revised edition of this book will want also to use the Revised Standard Version of the Bible.

schools and colleges and theological seminaries, and as refresher reading for the busy pastor who needs, from time to time, to take a fresh look at the contents of the New Testament as a whole.

The contributors to this volume are: James E. Bear, Professor of Christian Missions, Union Theological Seminary, Richmond, Virginia; Henry Wade DuBose, President, Assembly's Training School, Richmond, Virginia; Paul Leslie Garber, Professor of Bible, Agnes Scott College, Decatur, Georgia; Joseph M. Garrison, Pastor, Church of the Covenant, Greensboro, North Carolina; Felix B. Gear, Professor of Theology, Columbia Theological Seminary, Decatur, Georgia; and Patrick D. Miller, Pastor, Druid Hills Presbyterian Church, Atlanta, Georgia. Dr. DuBose wishes to make acknowledgment to Dr. Joseph M. Gettys, for valuable assistance, especially in preparation of the commentary on the Epistle to the Hebrews.

The work has been done in the full realization that the finished volume will contain a wide variety of guidance material because of two considerations: (1) the different sections of the Bible represent many types of literature which cannot be interpreted by a uniform pattern, and (2) six writers of such a work will obviously reflect their respective literary styles. Before submitting the manuscript for publication each writer was given an opportunity to read the whole, to revise his material if he wished to do so, and to make constructive suggestions for the revision of other sections. The volume, therefore, has had more than usual editorial study and revision.

I am greatly indebted to many friends, particularly to Mrs. Alma H. Clinevell, my efficient secretary for nine years, for her service in preparing the original manuscript; to Miss Mary Virginia Robinson of John Knox Press, for valuable suggestions in preparing the manuscript for publication; and to Mr. Robert A. Stratton, also of John Knox Press, for his symbolic illustrations.

Patrick H. Carmichael
Richmond, Virginia

CONTENTS

NEW TESTAMENT SURVEY

FELIX B. GEAR

NEW TESTAMENT SURVEY

NEW TESTAMENT SURVEY

I. THE MEANING OF THE NEW TESTAMENT

What does the term "New Testament" mean? We cannot give a satisfactory answer to this question without a clear understanding of the Old Testament. Let us, therefore, turn to it for a moment. There we find that the Hebrews thought of themselves as the "People of God." They believed that when they became his people at Sinai, he and they entered upon a mutual agreement, pact, or covenant. The conditions of this covenant were inscribed on tablets of stone and took the form of laws or commands. It was understood that if the people were to receive God's blessing and protection they were to observe the laws he gave them. In other words, he was to be their God and they were to be his people if they obeyed him. The term "covenant," then, in the Old Testament, as applied to this relation between God and his people means that God made a gracious and certain promise to them and held out the hope of a religious inheritance for them if they met the conditions set forth.

When we come to the New Testament, we find that the words "covenant" and "testament" are often used interchangeably. The New Testament writers carried forward the Old Testament usage of the term "covenant." They also added other meanings to it, thereby giving it a broader scope and a richer content. For example, the idea of "inheritance," as found in the promised blessings of the Old Testament, is a significant part of the covenant relationship between God and his people. In the New Testament, the notion of "inheritance" is greatly enriched by the conception of Sonship; "And if children, then heirs; heirs of God, and joint-heirs with Christ." (Rom. 8:17.)

The use of the word "testament" in the New Testament shows a similar process of enrichment taking place. Strictly speaking, a "testament" is a will which a person makes before his death and which is thereafter binding on those who survive. The further and deeper meaning given to this word by the New Testament writers is the idea of a bequest, something which is left by a will at death. Thus while the first or old covenant was dedicated with blood, the new covenant required the death of him who gave it to make it valid.

Still another idea attached to the word "testament" in the New Testament is that of "dispensation" or "regime." This carries with it the view that there were two eras in the history of the world, in each of which there was a "covenant" or "testament." The divine message of the first or old covenant was written on stone and we speak of it as the dispensation, regime, or era of law. The new covenant was stamped upon the hearts of men and was made effective by the death of Christ. It is usually called the dispensation of the gospel or of grace.

To sum up: the New Testament is the name given to those writings or documents which contain the assured promises of blessings given or willed to us by God and made effective and available for us by the death of Christ.

II. THE RELIGIOUS BACKGROUND OF THE NEW TESTAMENT

In order to understand the New Testament we need to know something about the religious background out of which it came, which was Jewish throughout. The ruling ideas of first-century Judaism will throw much light upon the New Testament. We shall consider four of these.

1. *Belief in One God*

Jews everywhere believed in one, and only one, God. This doctrine of the unity of God is called monotheism. The "Shema" expresses their faith in a single supreme God: "Hear, O Israel: The LORD our God is one LORD." (Deut. 6:4.) He made and ruled the world and was actively interested in man and the affairs of the world. He was the Father of his people and the Creator of each of them and of all. There was no other God.

Their belief in one God was in a sense a national or political monotheism. The view that God was their God was basic to their national as well as to their religious life. One of the worst features of this intensely patriotic conception of religion was the effect it had upon their idea of the relation of God and of Israel to the Gentile world. Regarding themselves as being particularly favored by God and as having special opportunities of knowing the true God, the Jews felt they were superior to other peoples racially, morally, intellectually, and religiously. Much of the teachings of Jesus and the writings of Paul should be studied in the light of this sense of superiority of the Jews.

2. *Salvation by Law*

The Jews also believed that salvation came to them through keeping the Law. It would not be an exaggeration to say that the Law was to them what Christ is to Christians. The Law was the link between the Jew and his God. It was his privilege and duty to obey the precepts of the Law. This was the only way he could serve or approach God. Judaism of the first century was a legal religion and its legalism was growing.

Ultimately, the Law was emptied of its real meaning, Judaism made it of no effect by traditions. (Mark 7:13.) Thus, in the time of Jesus, the gospel of salvation by law had lost its power, although it was still preached. The Law helped to increase the spirit of exclusiveness, pride, and contempt for the non-Jewish world. Those who no longer observed the Law—the publicans and sinners—were ostracized. Its system of rewards and punishments helped to make religion a sort of contract or a bargain, obscuring the nature of sin. Both Jesus and Paul opposed the legalism of Judaism.

3. *Expectation of a Messiah*

Another outstanding feature of Judaism was the expectation of a Messiah. The hope of a Messiah took varying forms in the successive centuries of development. Two different aspects of the Messiah's person and work are set forth in the Old Testament. He is thought of as an ideal king who will save them from all enemies and whose reign is to be one of universal and endless peace and prosperity. Again, he is described as a deliverer for Israel who accomplishes his task by sacrifice, suffering, and death, and is spoken of as the "Suffering Servant of Jehovah." But Judaism of the first century emphasized only the former of these two aspects of the person and mission of the Messiah. Jewish literature of that period apparently makes no reference whatever to an atoning death of the Messiah. If we study the New Testament with this in mind, we can more readily understand the hostility to Jesus on the part of the recognized religious leaders as well as the perplexity of his disciples when he spoke of the spiritual nature of the Kingdom of God and of his suffering and death as necessary to its establishment.

4. *The Kingdom of God*

The great dream of Judaism was that the Kingdom of God should be set up at the coming of the Messiah. We find the essence of the idea of the Kingdom of God in the Old Testament. The government of Israel was regarded ideally as a theocracy, that is, ruled by God. Israel, then, was the Kingdom of God. While this view was largely lost sight of after the monarchy was established, the thought that God was the true King of Israel was never completely forgotten. The great ethical prophets of the Old Testament said that the Kingdom of God would come only through repentance and renewal. In the dark days of the Exile, the prophets regarded the re-establishment of the reign of God as the only effective way to relieve the sufferings of the nation. As time passed and the Kingdom of God did not come, the nature of the dream of the future was radically changed. It was expanded from its simple form into an elaborate, colorful, highly imaginative conception and is found in a type of literature known as "apocalyptic." (See section on the Revelation.)

The substance of the preaching of Jesus was "the gospel of the Kingdom." The phrase "kingdom of heaven" is used in the New Testament by Matthew only, and is an exact equivalent of the phrase, "kingdom of God." The use of the conception of "the kingdom of God" by Jesus has given it a place of supreme importance, but we should be careful to learn what use he made of it, and what he meant by it.

III. THE WRITING OF THE NEW TESTAMENT

1. *The Bible of the Early Church*

The Old Testament was the only Bible of the early church for more than a century, but from the beginning the sayings of Jesus carried authority and were soon placed on the same level as the Scriptures of the Old Testament. For a long time after the death of Jesus his followers would hardly feel the need of having what he said and did in written form. Those who had been with him had vivid memories of his earthly life and others could learn about him from those who had known him. Early Christian preaching consisted largely of the presentation of the facts about his life, teaching, death, and resurrection, with a view to showing that these were in fulfillment of Old Testament prophecy.

2. *Some Books Written for Instruction and Evangelization*

As the gospel spread to other parts of the world, as a result of persecution and through the missionary efforts of the apostles, witnesses to the saving power and purpose of the living Christ were found among many who had never known or seen Jesus in the flesh at all. Also, after several years, the number of those who had firsthand knowledge of the facts of his life and ministry was reduced as old age and death removed them from the scene of action. If the large host of followers of Christ were to learn fully about him it was necessary to have the facts about him set down in writing by those who knew him or could get the information from eyewitnesses. It was thus that the first three books of our New Testament came into existence. They were written primarily for the purpose of instruction and evangelization. With a similar purpose in mind, Luke wrote the book of Acts showing the growth of Christian missions from a small beginning in Jerusalem until God's message of redemption was carried throughout the Roman Empire.

3. *Some to Combat Errors*

Some of the books of the New Testament were written to combat errors which sprang up in the Christian church. Paul states the Christian faith, in his letter to the Colossians, so as to show that it is superior to, and incompatible with, the doctrines of Gnosticism which denied the real humanity of Jesus and taught the worship of angels. (See pages 42-43.) He also attacks Jewish legalism and heathen practices.

Word had apparently reached the author of the Gospel of John that both the deity and humanity of our Lord were being denied and that the unity of his Person was being called into question. John writes to refute such errors and to show that Jesus is the Christ and that those who believe on him shall have life eternal. (See pages 31-34.) The ideas set forth in the First and Second Epistles of John show that they are concerned with exposing and curbing the falsity of the teaching of Gnosticism.

Somewhere in the early church, Christianity was attacked as a barren and inadequate faith. It was regarded as a religion without a revealed law, a sacrificial system, a priesthood, a temple, or a covenant relation to God. The Epistle to the Hebrews was written to meet such a situation and pictures Christ as the true Mediator between man and God and as the real fulfillment of the Old Testament types.

4. Some to Meet Problems

A large number of the books of the New Testament were produced to meet specific problems and to answer certain questions which arose in some of the churches. The Epistle of James, perhaps the first New Testament writing, counsels Jewish Christians who apparently believed that faith in Christ meant freedom from work instead of freedom for work. Paul's First and Second Epistles to the Thessalonians were necessary because of a misunderstanding of his teaching about the Second Coming of Christ and the failure to exercise proper discipline among the Christians at Thessalonica. The church at Corinth had split into factions, immorality had become a scandal, difficulties about marriage had arisen, relationships with pagans disturbed many, the purpose and nature of the Lord's Supper had been misunderstood, and Paul's authority as an apostle was called into question by some. These conditions made it necessary for

Paul to write First and Second Corinthians, to try to restore order there and to guide them in their perplexities.

5. Some to Meet Expanding Needs of the Growing Church

As Christianity expanded in organization and thought it became increasingly necessary for the apostles to keep in close touch with the churches they had founded. New converts often needed help; financial support and hospitality would be needed by the missionaries. Plans for future work, and instruction and encouragement for the leaders, became necessary.

Paul writes to Philemon in behalf of the slave Onesimus and urges him to receive his former slave as a brother in Christ. He sends a letter to the Philippians to thank them for their generous financial support sent to him while he was a prisoner at Rome.

In First and Second Timothy,* Paul makes plans for the further extension of the work of the gospel and for perpetuating the Christian movement after he had been removed. He writes Titus to carry on the task of instructing the converts and organizing the work in Crete. Paul writes the letter to the Romans in anticipation of a visit to Rome, on his way to Spain. While a prisoner at Rome, he writes the Epistle to the Ephesians, which shows that God is to be glorified in human history in Christ and the church.

The Third Epistle of John was written to commend Gaius for entertaining and supporting some missionaries who had gone forth "for the sake of the Name." John promises to attend to Diotrephes, who had opposed the missionaries and the group in the church who helped them.

6. Some to Strengthen Amidst Persecution

Christians suffered persecution from the beginning. Jewish opposition arose first, but as this new doctrine spread throughout the Roman Empire it met with hostility on every hand and many Christians were put to death. In view of this situation, Christians needed encouragement to remain true to the faith, unwavering in courage,

---

* Concerning the belief held by many scholars that the Pastoral Epistles, I and II Timothy and Titus, are not Pauline or not entirely so see pp. 44-45.

and strong in moral discipline. The Epistle of Jude, the First and Second Epistles of Peter, and Revelation grew out of an environment of hatred and constant danger and must have brought hope and encouragement to many who were called upon to suffer for the sake of the gospel.

This brief review of how the books of the New Testament came into existence enables us to see that the Holy Spirit was using the followers of Jesus to promote and preserve the growing movement of Christianity. The New Testament is the product of a growing church engaged in missionary evangelism. From this standpoint we should study and use it today. We can also see the varied ways in which the Holy Spirit, amid ignorance and opposition, sought to provide the teachings of Christianity for the further development of the church through the centuries.

IV. THE FORMATION OF THE NEW TESTAMENT

1. Early Use of the New Testament Writings

Perhaps you are wondering how the writings which we have been discussing came to be regarded as sacred and were finally added to the Old Testament Scriptures to form our Bible. At first the word "gospel" was not connected with a written book. The accounts of the life, work, and teaching of Jesus were spread by word of mouth for several years after his death, and were spoken of as the "gospel." As soon as this oral gospel was put into writing by Mark, Matthew, and Luke, their records were regarded as authoritative and soon began to be classed as sacred. Thus the church was beginning to develop a Scripture of its own, in addition to the Old Testament.

Early Christian worship was very much like the worship of the Jewish synagogue. It consisted of prayer, singing of a Psalm or a hymn, reading of Scripture, and an address or comments. When a letter from one of the apostles had been received it would be read at the worship service instead of having the address. It was often necessary to read it more than once in order to acquaint the hearers with its language and full meaning. In the course of time the custom of reading it at intervals became established, and because of its source it would be listened to with reverent attention. Ultimately, instead of taking the place of the address it would be read instead of an Old Testament passage, and time would be devoted to explaining certain parts to the congregation. Several such letters were in possession of churches, but as yet no attempt was made to collect them into one body of Scripture.

2. First Attempt to Form the New Testament

About the middle of the second century, a man by the name of Marcion drew up the first New Testament. He rejected the Old Testament and held that the God of the Jews was inferior to the God revealed in Christ and proclaimed by Paul. His Bible consisted of ten Epistles of Paul, omitting the pastoral letters, and the Gospel according to Luke. The church rejected this Bible, but saw the necessity of having some standard by which the teaching of the church could be guided. It soon became evident that the church must select the genuine writings which were to be used as the rule of faith and practice.

3. The Growth of the Canon

The process of forming what we call the "canon" of the New Testament, the list of books regarded as Scripture, lasted over two hundred years, being completed in A.D. 367. Leaders of Christian thought did not always agree on the books to be included in the New Testament. Some of those which were finally accepted were rejected for a while. Others which were ultimately rejected were temporarily regarded as entitled to a place in the canon. (For principles of selecting the books of the canon see Westminster Bible dictionary article, "Canon of the New Testament.")

Time has shown that the judgment of the early church was sound. The books which now stand in the New Testament contain those things which are vital and permanent in the teaching of Christianity. Their intrinsic worth won for them a lasting place in the Bible. Again we can see the Holy Spirit at work preserving for all time those writings which were produced by his presence and power in the lives of those who wrote them. That is what we understand by the statement that the Bible was written by men who were "taught by the Holy Ghost."

V. THE ARRANGEMENT OF THE NEW TESTAMENT

The New Testament is composed of twenty-seven books. They fall readily into four groups and may be classified as follows: (1) Gospels, (2) History, (3) Epistles, (4) Apocalypse. Their order of arrangement is not chronological, but fits in, more or less, to a general plan showing the beginning of Christianity, its expansion and development under the apostles, early Christian letters setting forth its doctrines and ideals, and finally the apocalyptic vision of its consummation. It was not until many centuries after the writing of the New Testament that the division into chapters and verses was made. While convenient for reference, this arrangement often obscures the meaning and interrupts the narrative. More recent versions of the Bible have placed the chapter and verse numbers on the margin.

1. Gospels

"Gospel" is the usual English translation of the Greek word which means "good tidings." The word "gospel" originally meant "story about God." In the New Testament, "good tidings" is the term applied to the message of salvation as preached by our Lord or others. It did not come to mean a written story of Christ's life and ministry until about the second century. The portion of the New Testament which contains the good news of God as revealed in the life, teachings, deeds, death, and resurrection of Christ is now universally called the "Gospels."

Synoptic Gospels

The Gospels are Matthew, Mark, Luke, and John. The first three are generally called "synoptic" and their authors "synoptists," because all of them give the same general view of the life and ministry of our Lord. The incidents recorded, their order of occurrence, and the language used, are very much the same throughout these three Gospels, and they have a similar point of view. The general aim of the Synoptists is to place before the reader a genuine and vivid picture of the gracious personality of Jesus Christ as he lived among men.

They show how his character, teaching, and service won the hearts of those who knew him until they gladly committed themselves to him in love and obedience.

The Fourth Gospel

The Gospel according to John does not give the same general account of the life of Christ, or the same point of view we find in the other Gospels. The aim of the fourth evangelist is different. He wrote after the rise of erroneous teaching and he aims definitely at establishing the true doctrine of the Person of Christ. He selects sayings and incidents from the life of Christ which show that he is the divine Son of God.

This Gospel may be called a sermon on the text, "And the Word was made flesh, and dwelt among us." (John 1:14.) He apparently takes it for granted that the other Gospels are well known and he omits most of the sayings and events which they give. Because of this, his Gospel forms a very valuable addition to the Synoptic record. As Irenaeus, a leader of the early church, puts it: "The Word, who was manifested to men, has given us the gospel under four aspects, but bound together by one Spirit."

2. *History*

The book of Acts naturally follows the Gospels. It is classed as "history" because it gives an account of how the Christian church came into being at Pentecost, and of how it grew until it reached to the far ends of the Roman Empire. With the exception of a few facts recorded in the Epistles of Paul, it is the only first-century authority for the momentous things which happened during the first thirty-five years after the ascension of our Lord. Without it we would be almost entirely in the dark about the origin and development of the early church. At best our knowledge of this phase of the history of the church is very inadequate.

3. *Epistles*

The third group of New Testament books is generally referred to as "Epistles" or "Letters." They are products of the pens of early Christian writers who were bearing testimony to their experience in Christ, extending their influence for him, and were concerned with defending and strengthening the faith, increasing the knowledge, and improving the character of those to whom they were writing, hoping thus to contribute to the building up of the church.

Pauline Epistles

Of the twenty-one Epistles in the New Testament, the first thirteen bear the name of Paul, and are called the "Pauline Epistles." They appear in the following order: Romans, First and Second Corinthians, Galatians, Ephesians, Philippians, Colossians, First and Second Thessalonians, First and Second Timothy, Titus, and Philemon. They were not written in this order, but their size and importance helped to determine their place in the New Testament.

Hebrews

The Epistle to the Hebrews is the fourteenth Epistle in the present arrangement of New Testament books. It has often been classed with the Pauline Epistles but we really do not know who wrote it. The King James Version of the Bible ascribes it to Paul, but this ascription is only in the title, which is not a part of the original work but was added later.

General Epistles

Seven Epistles are frequently included in the so-called "catholic" or "general" Epistles and form the last group of letters in the New Testament. They are probably given this title because they are addressed not to individuals, or particular churches, but to a group of churches in certain areas. These Epistles are: James; First and Second Peter; First, Second, and Third John; and Jude.

4. *Apocalypse*

Revelation, the last book in the New Testament, is unlike any of the others. It is placed in a class by itself and belongs to a type of literature called "apocalyptic." It was the product of suffering and persecution at the hands of a foreign power. Its aim was to bolster

up the faith, hope, and courage of a distressed people by holding before them the promise that deliverance by the hand of God was
forthcoming and that the righteous were to wait for it patiently. The
book of Daniel, in the Old Testament, is apocalyptic.

VI. THE FOUR GOSPELS

1. *General Aim*

The motive of the Gospel records is evangelistic throughout. Jesus
had told his followers to look to the future—to his return when he
would consummate his work and Kingdom. It was in view of this
expectation that the disciples sought to win men and women to a
faith in their Lord.

The fact that we have more than one Gospel account is probably
due to a desire to have a record of certain facts and events in the life
of our Lord which could be used in evangelism, in instruction, and
even in public worship. Because of this, we are not surprised
to find the Gospel accounts differing among themselves in emphasis
and approach. Yet the common subject of the Gospels gives them a
necessary unity of purpose and content—especially the Synoptics,
which cover largely the same phases of Christ's life and ministry.

2. *The Synoptic Problem*

One does not go far in the study of the Gospels without encounter-
ing what is called by New Testament students "The Synoptic Problem," which is the question of the relation of the Gospels to one another and their sources. Investigations in this field attempt to answer
such inquiries as the following: Which of the Gospels was written
first? Where did the writer of each Gospel get his material? Did
Matthew and Luke use the Gospel of Mark as a source of information? How are differences in the Gospel accounts of the same discourses and events to be explained? In short, the question of the relation of the Gospels to one another and their sources forms one of
the most interesting and difficult fields for study in the New Testament. (See Dummelow's commentary, pp. lxxxiii-lxxxv.)

3. Survey of the Synoptic Gospels

Matthew

Authorship. This Gospel is thought by some to have been compiled from various sources. In its present form, however, it clearly shows the work of a single writer. Mark's account was most likely the chief source for the narrative portions. Other material was added at appropriate intervals, but the order of events as given in Mark is followed fairly well throughout.

No mention is made of the name of the author in any of the Gospels, and there is no hint in Matthew as to who wrote it. From the beginning, tradition has ascribed it to Matthew, one of the twelve disciples of Jesus. Many think that Matthew did not write it in its present form since the author leaves the impression that he is relying on the observation of others and earlier documentary sources, whereas the Apostle Matthew would have written as an eyewitness.

We can be certain that the author was a Jewish Christian. The whole story is cast so in the Messianic pattern of thought that we cannot believe any other than a Jew could have done it. He stresses the Messianic function of Jesus, as the fulfillment of Old Testament prophecy, and the teaching concerning "last things" as no other Gospel writer does. Also, he uses Jewish terms constantly, such as "the land of Israel," "the God of Israel," and "the kingdom of heaven," rather than "the kingdom of God," as found especially in Mark and Luke. While he sets forth the universality of the Kingdom, he emphasizes the idea that it was for the Jew first; and he gives the Law a prominent place. Our conclusion, therefore, is that the disciple by that name, if not directly responsible for the Gospel as we now have it, had a great deal to do with writing it, such as supplying the discourses and sayings of Jesus.

Readers. The Gospel was intended for Jewish Christians outside of Palestine. That the readers were Jewish is obvious from the author's portrayal of Jesus as the Jewish Messiah who was in accord with Old Testament prophecy. The explanation of certain terms and customs shows, however, that the author expected to have some readers who were not familiar with Jewish history and practices.

Motive. Matthew presents Jesus as the fulfillment of the history and principles of Israel as a theocracy, as set forth in the Old Testament. At the same time, he makes it clear that Jesus does not fit into the current Messianic hopes and expectations. As he gives a true picture of the life and work of Jesus, the error of Judaism is revealed in contrast to the Kingdom of God which is to be world-wide in its scope. The Kingdom of God—or of heaven—was not to be limited by national or racial identity; it was to include all who might seek to enter the Kingdom. This community or society of the redeemed is the "church." Jesus, then, is shown as having come to establish the Kingdom of God among men, and its visible expression is the "church of the Living God."

Time and Place. As to when the Gospel was written, we can say little of a positive nature. The prevailing opinion is that it was written shortly before the destruction of Jerusalem, in A.D. 70. We do not know the place of writing.

Contents. It is important to remember that Matthew follows the general scheme of Mark's Gospel, but groups his material together so as to illustrate certain features of the life and work of Jesus. In relating events given in Mark, the first Gospel reduces the narrative to its shortest possible form. (For example, Matthew 8:28-34; Mark 5:1-20.) Matthew's groupings are different from Mark's, and he stresses different aspects in the life of Jesus.

Matthew's account of the life, sayings, and work of Jesus may be stated briefly as follows: As the Messiah, Jesus descends from Abraham (chs. 1—2); his baptism (ch. 3); his Galilean ministry (chs. 4—16); his conception of the true Messiahship (chs. 17—20); events and discourses during his stay in Jerusalem (chs. 21—25); and the tragic ending on the cross, the resurrection, and the new beginning of the work of the Kingdom (chs. 26—28). The story closes with the double note—the universal Kingdom and the ever-present Christ.

Mark

The Author. The Jewish name of the author of the second Gospel was John. In Gentile and Christian circles he was called Mark. His mother's home was used as a meeting place for early Christians in

Jerusalem (Acts 12:12), and it is thought that Peter lodged at her home when in Jerusalem. Mark was undoubtedly well acquainted with Peter. It has been suggested that he became a Christian through his association with Peter.

Mark is mentioned several times in the New Testament. He was a cousin of Barnabas and accompanied Paul and Barnabas on their first missionary journey. He left them at Perga. We do not know why he did not continue with them. When Paul and Barnabas were planning their second trip, Paul refused to allow Mark to go with them. Paul and Barnabas quarreled over this and separated. Mark went with Barnabas to Cyprus. Because of this, some have thought that Mark may have been originally from Cyprus. Later, however, Paul regards Mark in a different light and writes of him as "useful to me for ministering." (II Tim. 4:11.)

According to tradition, Mark was an interpreter of Peter in much of his missionary work. Peter refers to him as "my son." Mark's account of the life and work of Jesus is thought to have been derived mostly from Peter. This would explain the graphic style of his Gospel. He probably recorded the events as Peter described them to him, or as he heard Peter preach them.

Readers. The second Gospel was written for Gentile Christians who were not only unfamiliar with the language and customs of Palestine, but whose acquaintance with the Old Testament was apparently very slight. Mark explains Aramaic terms and uses some Latin terms which are peculiar to him. He does not quote the Old Testament as does Matthew's Gospel which is addressed to the Jews. He says little about the Law and Prophets. Just where these Gentile Christians were we do not know. Rome is frequently mentioned as a possibility.

Motive. Mark presents Jesus to his Gentile readers in such a way that they will understand, appreciate, and accept him who came as a ministering Servant to give his life a ransom for many. He portrays the actual reality of Jesus' wonderful life. He emphasizes the marvelous deeds he performed and their effects on those who witnessed them. Mark gives very little of what Jesus said, but much of what he did; nineteen miracles are recorded and only nine parables are given. Matthew relates twenty-one miracles and twenty parables. Luke has twenty-two miracles and twenty-seven parables.

Time and Place. There is no indication where the Gospel was written, but tradition states that Mark wrote it at Rome either shortly before or after Peter's death. For other reasons it is believed to have been written before the fall of Jerusalem in A.D. 70. Perhaps a date just prior to Peter's martyrdom in A.D. 64 best suits all the conditions.

Contents. Mark arranges the material of his narrative so as to depict the general progress of the ministry of Jesus and follows chronologically the sequence of individual events. This Gospel contains only about thirty verses peculiar to itself. He alone gives the parable of the seed growing secretly (4:26-29), the healing of the blind man at Bethsaida (8:22-26), and the story of the young man who fled from the soldiers at the time of Jesus' arrest (14:51-52).

This Gospel tells us nothing about the birth and infancy of Jesus. It opens with the preparatory work of John the Baptist and a brief account of the baptism and temptation of Jesus. (1:1-13.) Mark then tells of the ministry of Jesus in and near Capernaum. (1:14—4:34.) The scene of his ministry shifts to the other side of the Sea of Galilee and for a while he works on first one side of the lake and then the other. (4:35—7:23.) He spends some time, we do not know how long, in the neighborhood of Tyre and Sidon (7:24-30), after which he returns to the eastern side of the Sea of Galilee, "through the midst of the borders of Decapolis" (7:31—8:21). He then moves on to Bethsaida, where he restores the sight of a blind man. (8:22-26.) His disciples accompany him on the journey to Caesarea Philippi, where the "Great Confession" of Peter takes place and the disclosure of the true nature of his Messiahship and Kingdom is made to the disciples. (8:27—9:29.) Again passing through Galilee, he begins his last journey to Jerusalem, traveling the road which runs north and south, east of the Jordan River. (9:30—10:52.) After his arrival in Jerusalem, which is usually called the "Triumphal Entry," the significant events of the Passion or Holy Week follow rapidly upon each other, leading to the tragedy of the cross. (11:1—15:47.) Finally, we are told about his resurrection and his appearance to many of his followers. (Ch. 16.)

Luke

Author. We are told nothing about the author in the third Gospel. It is almost universally acknowledged, however, that the same person wrote Luke's Gospel and the book of Acts. (See discussion on authorship of Acts, page 35.)

Readers. The third Gospel, unlike the others, is addressed to an individual, by the name of Theophilus. He evidently was a Gentile, for the Gospel appears to have been written for one who was not familiar with either Jewish customs or Palestinian geography. Tradition places him at Antioch in Syria, but we have no information about this. From the author's manner of addressing Theophilus as "most excellent," it is frequently supposed that he was a man of rank. While written primarily for an individual, the author no doubt expected that the book would eventually be useful for a wider circle of Gentile readers.

Motive. Theophilus had received some information about Christianity and was apparently favorably inclined toward it, giving some attention to its claims. Luke attempts to supply him with certain and further knowledge of the matters regarding which he had been instructed in order to win him fully to the new faith by giving him, in their full historical setting, the Gospel stories which he himself has learned from others more intimately acquainted with them.

Time and Place. We cannot determine the date of composition with certainty. It is placed later than Mark, since Luke is thought to have used that Gospel as one of his sources. Also it was written before Acts, to which it serves as an introduction.

Many hold that it could not have been written until after the fall of Jerusalem, which would place the date of writing shortly after A.D. 70.

About all we can say about the place of writing is that it was probably outside of Palestine. This conclusion is based upon the fact that the writer was a Gentile and also upon the Gentile coloring of the book.

Contents. The Gospel opens with a preface which states the purpose of the writer and the sources of his material. (1:1-4.) The infancy and boyhood of Jesus are described with unsurpassed literary beauty and skill. (1:5—2:52.) The ministry of John the Baptist is then shown to prepare the way for the work of Jesus. (3:1-20.) Jesus' fitness and preparation for his ministry are given in the description of his baptism, his pedigree, and his temptation. (3:21—4:13.) The author tells about the Galilean ministry somewhat in detail. (4:14—9:50.) This is followed by a record of his later ministry, largely in Perea. (9:51—19:28.) (We are not given exact information as to location and dates in this section. Many of the incidents mentioned in this portion of the Gospel may belong to other periods of the ministry.) Luke describes in vivid fashion the last visit to Jerusalem and the Passion Week. (19:28—23:56.) The narrative closes with the story of the resurrection and a brief statement of the ascension. (Ch. 24.)

4. The Fourth Gospel

Relation to the Synoptics. We have already indicated that there is quite a difference between the Gospel of John and the Synoptic Gospels. In the Fourth Gospel, John the Baptist is reported as giving more explicit testimony to the Messiahship of Jesus. Jesus is also shown as less reluctant to let it be known. The type of miracle most frequently found in the first three Gospels—the casting out of devils —is not mentioned in John. He regards Christ's miracles as "signs" or "works" which illustrate or throw light upon the doctrine or spiritual principle before him. Only eight miracles are given.

This record is distinguished from the other Gospels in that the writer intends to convey a hidden spiritual meaning beneath the actual words of his narrative. He gives an interpretation, for Christian experience, of the life and teachings of Christ. Much of the mysterious charm of this Gospel flows from the constant use of symbolism. The reader feels that more is suggested than is seen on the surface. We should study it in the light of this fact. Because of this feature it is sometimes difficult to understand, although it is written in very simple language.

General Characteristics. The Fourth Gospel is no doubt the most familiar and best-loved book in the Bible. Few books have exercised so wide an influence as this. The only other literature like it is the Epistles of John. Much of its influence and popularity are due to the author's exceptional ability to express the profoundest ideas in language of childlike simplicity. The peculiar union of simplicity and profundity creates the impression of sublimity. This Gospel has from the beginning been spoken of as a sublime writing. Even as early as the second century the accepted symbol for its author was a soaring eagle.

Authorship. A continuous strain in tradition has assigned to the Apostle John the authorship of this Gospel, but few sacred writings have been more subject to controversy in modern times. Some assert that, almost beyond question, John the "beloved disciple" wrote it. Others are just as certain that he did not. The author has so carefully concealed his identity that it is exceedingly difficult to discover who he was. The church, however, has somewhat tenaciously held on to the tradition that the Apostle John wrote the Fourth Gospel. What further light may be thrown upon this question by future study and research remains to be seen. Pending such discoveries, the traditional view of the authorship of the Fourth Gospel will continue to live. (For discussion of authorship, see the Westminster Bible dictionary and Dummelow's commentary.)

Readers. We have no specific information about those for whom the Gospel of John was written. It is generally inferred (20:30-31) that they were already Christians. It seems evident, too, that the writer had previously come in contact with them in his work and that he attempted to bring them into a more vital faith in Christ by this interpretation of Christ's life.

Motive. The nature of the narrative convinces us that the author was not trying to write a history, or a biography of Christ—it is too meager for that. His purpose is clearly revealed to be religious. (20: 30-31.) While this is also true of the other Gospel writers, this author stresses the religious motive in a peculiar fashion by presenting the personality of Christ as it has influenced his own spiritual life. Here it is not his miraculous works, or the people's enthusiasm for him, but Jesus' own consciousness of his divine nature and mission which stands out so clearly. Thus the writer's main object is to produce faith in Jesus as the Messiah and the Son of God and to give what he conceives to be the proper view of his person and work. He emphasizes our Lord's true deity and true humanity. The former was called into question by Ebionite tendencies, the latter by Docetic teachings. Further, he emphasizes the unity of Christ's person as against Cerinthus, who held that Jesus was a mere man upon whom the heavenly son of God came at the baptism. But to John, the consciousness of Jesus was an unbroken stream reaching back into eternity: "Before Abraham was born, I am." (8:58; see also 6:33 ff.)

Time and Place. Ancient authorities are agreed that this Gospel was written at Ephesus about A.D. 90, or perhaps a little earlier. There is nothing in the Gospel itself that throws any light upon the place of writing, but if it were written toward the close of the first Christian century, as is commonly supposed, it is unlikely that it was written in Palestine.

Contents. First, we should note some of the distinctive religious ideas of John's Gospel. "Eternal life" is regarded as a present possession as well as a future hope. "Judgment" is something that takes place *now,* and separates the friends of God from his enemies. He also makes a peculiar combination of the passion, resurrection, and ascension of Christ into one complete conception of which the chief feature is "glory." (E.g., 13:31-32.) He also develops more fully the doctrine of the Holy Spirit than do the Synoptics. The Gospel opens with a Prologue which declares Christ to be the eternal Word who revealed God and imparted salvation to those who believed. (1:1-18.) The rest of the book may be regarded as a testimony or witness to this revelation. We have the opening testimonies of John the Baptist and those of Jesus himself to his first disciples. (1:19—2:11.) He reveals himself in a series of deeds, and in discourses to inquirers or to his enemies. (2:12—12:50.) The supreme revelation of Christ is made in connection with his death and resurrection. (13:1—21:25.)

Throughout the dramatic presentation of this revelation, John shows that the response is twofold: there are faith and unbelief, or acceptance and rejection. The mission of Jesus is the climax of God's self-revelation. Those who believe and accept him receive light and come to know the highest truth. They also receive that life which consists in spiritual union with God. Thus they attain the supreme good in this life and everlasting salvation. From this simple but profound story we are able to see that in the human Jesus there was the eternal Son of God whose person, teaching, and redeeming work enable us to see God and enjoy eternal life in fellowship with him. "These [things] are written, that ye might believe that Jesus is the Christ, the Son of God; and that believing ye might have life in his name." (20:31.)

VII. THE ACTS OF THE APOSTLES

1. *Title*

We do not know how the fifth book of the New Testament got its name. In fact, different titles have been given it, such as "Acts," "Acts of Apostles," and "Acts of All the Apostles." It gives a detailed account of the work of only two of the Apostles—Peter and Paul. It mentions more briefly John, James the Son of Zebedee, Stephen, Philip, Barnabas, Timothy, and Silas. Thus it is generally believed that the title, as we now have it, was a later addition and was not a part of the original writing.

2. *Purpose*

Anyone who reads the Gospel according to Luke and Acts will be impressed with the fact that they were written by the same author and that they belong together, Acts being a continuation of the narrative of the Gospel. The author describes his earlier work as a "treatise . . . concerning all that Jesus *began* both to do and to teach, until the day in which he was received up." (Acts 1:1-2.) This is exactly what the Gospel according to Luke does, and Acts begins by explaining and expanding the closing sentences of that Gospel.

The aim, then, of his first work was to tell what "Jesus *began* to do and to teach." We should look for the second work to give only what the disciples *began* to do and teach after Jesus left them. We may, therefore, expect Acts to be only a history of *beginnings*. A study of its contents shows us that it is a work of this character. Jesus, before his ascension, charted the course of the preaching of the gospel. (Acts 1:8). In less than fifty years after the death of Jesus, his gospel had spread over Palestine and Asia Minor and had been carried by travelers and missionaries across the Aegean Sea to Greece and over the Mediterranean to Rome. It was beginning to reach out to the "uttermost part of the earth," expanding through the energy of the Spirit.

3. Author

The Gospel of Luke and the book of Acts were ascribed to Luke by the general voice of the church as far back as we are able to go. The writer of Acts was a traveling companion of Paul's and uses the first person plural in four different places in the narrative. (16: 10-17; 20:5-15; 21:1-18; 27:1—28:16.) These passages are known as the "we sections," or "diary passages," and are of value in establishing the authorship of the book because Luke fits into the general picture better than anyone else known to us. Paul refers to him as "the beloved physician." (Col. 4:14.) The accurate and frequent use of medical terms in the Gospel and Acts indicates that the writer possessed special knowledge in this field. Paul, as we know, was subject to sudden attacks of illness, and the company of a physician on his long journeys would be valuable to him, probably necessary.

The Third Gospel and Acts are connected in several ways. Both are addressed to "Theophilus," perhaps some well-known person of Luke's acquaintance. The two accounts belong together—the Gospel giving the story of Jesus' ministry, and Acts that of the spread of his Kingdom. Both were written from the point of view of a Gentile Christian who stresses the universality of the gospel of Christ. The style and language of the two books are notably alike.

4. Date

According to the date we have assigned to the writing of the Gospel according to Luke, we naturally assume that Acts was written toward the close of the decade A.D. 70-80.

5. Contents

The contents and arrangement of Acts grow out of the author's purpose, which was, as we have seen, to set forth the process by which the church has grown from a small beginning to a world-wide power. His design is not to give a complete history, but merely to select a number of important events to show the reader how Christianity grew in a hostile and pagan environment. There must have been many more incidents known to him which he had to omit as he chose those that would illustrate most aptly the various stages by which Christianity moved from Jerusalem to Rome.

The arrangement of the book is very simple. There are six distinct sections, each of them closing with a statement which sums up the progress made and points forward to the next one. These sections are as follows: (1) The origin of the church at Jerusalem (1:1—6:7); (2) The spread of Christianity in Palestine (6:8—9:31); (3) The growth from Palestine to Antioch in Syria (9:32—12:24); (4) The expansion from Syria to Asia Minor (12:25—16:5); (5) Paul's achievements in Macedonia and Greece (16:6—19:20); (6) The events which led to Paul's work in Rome (19:21—28:31).

VIII. THE PAULINE EPISTLES

1. *Introduction*

All of Paul's Epistles, with the exception of Philemon and the Pastoral Epistles, were addressed to churches rather than to individuals. They are genuine, personal, friendly letters which deal with actual situations. Their style and contents vary according to the needs of the readers for whom they are intended. Before their meaning can become clear to us, therefore, we have to know something about the position of the persons or churches he had in mind when he wrote the various Epistles.

These letters are the result of the vast program of missionary work conducted by Paul which rendered it impossible to deal with each individual or situation in person. They were doubtless written with care and after much thought. He intended that they be read aloud at the meeting of the church. Thus they were really public documents which had to be prepared carefully and phrased in language that would hold the attention and interest of the listeners. Even today, we cannot fully appreciate their beauty and eloquence until we hear them read out by a finished speaker. They give us the ripest fruits of one of the world's greatest minds.

2. The Order of Composition

Paul may have written some Epistles besides those we now have. Some think that most of the letters he wrote are now entirely lost. It is also possible that some portions of this lost correspondence have found their way into some of the letters we now possess. The surviving letters cover only about ten years of his missonary work. He was probably around fifty years of age when he wrote the first letter that has come down to us. The first twenty years of his life as a Christian are largely unknown to us. What development or changes took place in his thought during those years we have no way of knowing.

It is important to place his Epistles as nearly as we can in the order in which they were written. The information which they contain about his life and about conditions in the early church becomes more valuable to us when we read them in the light of their date. We cannot always be certain that we have the true order of the Epistles, but they are usually arranged according to certain periods in the latter part of Paul's life. The most common sequence is as follows: (1) Missionary Epistles—I and II Thessalonians, Galatians, I and II Corinthians, Romans; (2) Prison Epistles—Colossians, Philemon, Ephesians, Philippians; (3) The later Epistles—I and II Timothy, and Titus.

The incidental nature of his writings may lead us to think that they do not form a consistent and complete pattern of thought. Yet there does run through them one master purpose, an all-inclusive conception of human life and of the things of God. They express the supreme passion of a man whose sole aim was to "lay hold on that for which I was laid hold on by Christ Jesus."

3. Style of the Epistles

The New Testament is unique among the sacred writings of the world in that it is so largely composed of letters. This form of sacred writing is definitely the product of a new spiritual life and era, and deals with truth in the concrete experiences of life rather than in an abstract way. Here we have revealed the inner experiences and processes of the souls of their authors. They are burning and heart-throbbing messages to other Christians of that period. Their object is almost always personal. They relate the vital truths of early Christian experiences and the basic teaching of this new way of life to all believers. It was this specific aim which gave rise to this form of communication in the early church. This may be seen from the way in which, after the salutation in each letter, Paul usually gives the doctrinal basis on which he builds the practical duties of the daily life of the Christian. These are then followed by the personal messages, affectionate greetings, and directions necessary as each situation is addressed.

Paul had no doubt known the Greek language from childhood. He uses the language of the street, rather than the literary Greek of the times. But underneath the Greek culture was the spirit of a Jew. He knew well and often used the Old Testament, which he probably studied in the Greek translation. His imagery is that of the busy life of the cities and of the multitudes. He could and did change the style of expression to suit those to whom he was writing. He could produce stately and measured argument, scathing criticism, masterly defense, affectionate expression, frankness, spontaneity, and familiarity. He could comfort and encourage, warn and admonish, rebuke, and even threaten with punishment.

4. Content of Pauline Epistles

The content of Paul's Epistles may be arranged as follows: personal, doctrinal, ethical, administrative, and devotional. He blends and uses these various elements with perfect freedom. He writes mainly on doctrine in Romans. The personal element is predominant in II Corinthians, Philippians, and Philemon. We find doctrine and ethics fairly well balanced in II Thessalonians, Colossians, and Ephesians. In Galatians, doctrine is uppermost, but he unites the personal, doctrinal, and moral elements.

If you will read II Thessalonians and II Corinthians—the former stresses doctrine and the latter the personal element—as you would a letter from a friend, it will give you a good idea of the way in which Paul fashioned the form of his letters to their subject matter. Perhaps you should first try to make your own outline of each letter, and understand as clearly as possible the more difficult passages, so that you may get a complete impression of the entire Epistle. We should never lose sight of the fact that most of them were addressed to individuals or churches Paul had known for some time.

5. Characteristics of the Epistles

Let us look briefly at each of Paul's Epistles, noting the characteristics of each. We shall discuss them in the groupings and order given above.

Missionary Epistles

A.D. 50-57

I Thessalonians. This is probably the earliest of Paul's Epistles— written during the period A.D. 50-52. It was written to the church at Thessalonica, which he founded on his second missionary journey. He was in Corinth when he wrote, possibly only a few months after leaving Thessalonica. Timothy had just come from this city, bringing good news of the faithfulness of the church, but pointing out the weaknesses in this infant church. He reported a tendency to neglect their daily work, thinking the Second Coming of Christ was imminent; the prevalence of moral impurity; anxieties over the fact that those who had died would miss the glories of the Kingdom which Christ would bring with him; and friction within the church between officers and those with miraculous gifts. This accounts for the general outline of the Epistle.

II Thessalonians. This Epistle is assigned to the same period, A.D. 50-52, since it follows shortly after the first letter. We find the same problems in the church, but they have become more serious, particularly with regard to the Second Coming of Christ and the neglect of labor. He tells them that the advent of the Lord is not to be expected now, and that a falling away from the faith and the disclosure of the "man of sin" (lawlessness) will precede the Lord's return.

Galatians. An extended debate has been carried on among

scholars about what churches Paul addresses in this Epistle. The date of the Epistle depends also on the churches addressed; some scholars place the date as early as A.D. 49, while others date it in A.D. 53, 55 or 56, or even as late as 58. For a discussion of destination and date see the Dummelow commentary.

Galatians is of immense value to us for a number of reasons: (1) It tells us much about the life of Paul we would not otherwise have known, and when studied in the light of the record of his life in Acts it helps us to get a better idea of his life and work. (2) We see that his views on circumcision for Gentile Christians were in general accord with the opinion of the older apostles. (3) Since his doctrine of salvation by faith alone in Galatians is in such perfect agreement with the view set forth in Romans, we understand more clearly that he regarded Judaism as a wrong interpretation of the Old Testament and thus paved the way for making Christianity a world religion rather than a Jewish sect. (4) It is the Magna Charta of Christian liberty for all time.

The Epistle to the Galatians is the product of heated controversy which threatened to destroy the unity of the early church and upon the outcome of which the fate of Christianity depended. The real issue put briefly is: Shall Christianity remain a Jewish sect or become a world religion? Judaizing teachers among the Galatians were saying that observance of the laws of Moses was necessary for Christians. They attacked Paul's authority and charged him with inconsistency in preaching Gentile freedom from the law. They declared his view of salvation to be false. With great intensity of feeling and vigor of argument Paul pens this letter in defense of himself and above all in defense of the gospel he preached.

I Corinthians. Paul founded the church at Corinth on his second missionary journey. While he was in Ephesus, news had come to him that things in Corinth were not going so well. He had already written them a letter, containing instructions about marriage and morals. This letter has not been preserved. He had sent Timothy to Corinth to help clear up the situation. But when he got word that certain parties had arisen within the church he wrote I Corinthians immediately. He takes up in order the practical and doctrinal questions which were giving them trouble. This Epistle was probably written in A.D. 55 or 56.

II Corinthians. Unusual difficulties face us in studying this letter. Many scholars think that chapters 10—13 were written after I Corinthians, and that chapters 1—9 form a letter which he wrote after he learned the effect of the stand he took in his message found in chapters 10—13. This is an interesting study and should be pursued further in commentaries and articles on II Corinthians. The tone of this letter is quite different from that of the first. Paul refers to things not mentioned in the first letter. He writes as though a critical period in the relationship between him and the Corinthian church has been safely passed. Paul is apparently under an intense strain over perils confronting them and is anxious lest the Corinthians forsake him. It was written about eighteen months after First Corinthians.

Romans. This is the longest, most characteristic and comprehensive, as well as the most important letter Paul wrote. It fittingly comes first in his Epistles of the New Testament for it serves as an excellent introduction to his teaching and gives us a summary of his thought. It was addressed to the church at Rome, the capital of the Gentile world, which he had planned to visit. It prepares the way for his coming as here he makes known to them the peculiar turn he has given the gospel as the Apostle to the Gentiles.

He is thought to have written it from Corinth, toward the close of his third missionary journey, about A.D. 56. He had long intended to preach in Rome (1:13; 15:23), but his duties had made this impossible. Now he plans a trip to Jerusalem to carry the contribution for the needy saints and expects to go from there to Spain by way of Rome. This is a momentous epoch in his life. His mission to the Gentiles thus far has been marked by bitter opposition, controversy, and misunderstanding. Jewish pride, prejudice, and legalism have followed him everywhere and he has the enmity of many. Yet he has made remarkable progress. His horizon now extends beyond Jewish limits, partly as a result of Jewish obstinacy, and partly because his vision has grown and his insight deepened. He must now preach to the western part of the Empire.

Romans is a book of intense passion and unique power. The heroic spirit of the writer, his universal outlook, the note of triumph over controversy and misunderstanding, his invincible urge to greater conquests, and profound insight into human nature, combine to make it one of the greatest literary masterpieces of all time as well as a religious document of unsurpassed value. Paul is at his best in Romans.

A careful reading of chapters 1—8 will disclose that Paul is here stating positively what he more or less debated negatively and by argument in Galatians, and which I and II Corinthians took for granted. In chapters 9—11, he grapples with the problem raised by the rejection of the Gospel on the part of the Jews, who should have come first in acceptance—a problem which gave him serious concern and which stood as a barrier to his Gentile efforts. In chapters 12—16 he makes practical application of his doctrine to moral, social, and civil life—urging that the church bring everything under the all-embracing law of love. He concludes with personal and local touches and messages.

The Prison Epistles

Colossians. In about the year 62, Paul received word from Epaphras that a false and dangerous teaching was growing up in the church at Colossae. Although, so far as we know, Paul had never preached there, he had many friends in Colossae, and he was naturally interested in protecting one of the churches from error. Hence this letter.

This false doctrine was essentially Jewish in character, but it was not simply the old Jewish legalism Paul had fought for so long. Some see in this heresy the forerunner to Gnosticism. Stress was laid upon sacred seasons, the Sabbath, the new moon, the feast day; and certain meats and drinks were forbidden. Circumcision and observance of the Law of Moses and the tradition of men were regarded as necessary. Adherents to this view felt unworthy to worship God directly and worked out a detailed scheme of angelic beings and mediators. The worship of angels tended to degrade Christ from his true position as Creator of the universe and head of the church, and may have been a product of later Judaism. Immediate exposure of the falsity and weakness of this enemy to the faith was essential.

Paul deals with it by showing them that their Christian experience has been such as to prove that the worship of these creatures is useless. Christ is quite sufficient to supply everything needed for a full experience of salvation. His relation to God, the universe, and the church gives him a unique place of supremacy and pre-eminence. Worship of angels and worship of Christ cannot go together.

Philemon. Paul evidently had a great capacity for friendship. About one hundred people are mentioned by name in his letters. In his letter to Philemon, he opens his heart and writes to him as any friend would write to another. Philemon had become a Christian somewhere under Paul's ministry. Apparently a man of wealth, he was noted for his charity, hospitality to Christians, and zeal in spreading the gospel. Onesimus was Philemon's slave. He had run away and gone to Rome where Paul was a prisoner. He found Paul there and was brought to faith in Christ. Paul sent him back to his former owner and wrote Philemon this brief but valuable letter. It was written in the same circumstances and sent at the same time as Colossians, about A.D. 62. It is an appeal to a master in behalf of his slave.

Ephesians. This was probably a circular letter addressed to all the churches of the province of Asia. Ephesus being the chief city, the letter naturally came to be regarded as sent to the church there. It was probably written about A.D. 62, about the same time Paul wrote Colossians, and sent by Tychicus, who also carried the letter to the Colossians. These two letters show similarity of language and thought, and it is probable that Ephesians followed closely after the writing of Colossians, and carries the thought further.

Paul's theme in Ephesians is the establishment of the church considered as the full number of the redeemed. He appears to sum up his previous teaching so as to show the purpose of God in the mission of Christ, his Son, which was to redeem his chosen people and declare to all the universe the riches of his grace. It is Paul's most complete statement of the entire purpose of God in human history.

Philippians. Paul established the church at Philippi on his second missionary journey. He found there the warmth of friendship, depth of sincerity, and zeal for the gospel which made this little group of Christians stand out like a beacon light. More than others, they were grateful and devoted to him. At the first, Lydia took him and his helpers into her home. Her generosity seemed to be contagious in Philippi. They sent Paul aid on two different occasions while he was traveling.

Once again their hearts had turned to him in loving helpfulness. Epaphroditus had been sent to him in Rome with some money and was instructed to remain there and help him. He became ill and got homesick, so Paul sent him back, and this letter with him. News and greetings as well as financial help had been brought to Paul by Epaphroditus, and no doubt Paul had written to or heard from the Philippians since then. Thus Paul learned of their anxiety over Epaphroditus, as well as about himself.

There seem to have been no serious difficulties in Philippi; no false teachings, no scandalous conduct, and no bitter enemies. Perhaps there was a lack of complete harmony among the leaders, and a need for further enlightenment concerning the gospel and the Christian way of life. The Epistle was written primarily to thank the Philippians for their gift, but Paul takes the opportunity to tell them about himself and warn them against error. Here we have a pastor writing to his flock. In addition to the thought it contains, it is valuable because of the light it throws on his situation at Rome.

The Pastoral Epistles

Before taking up each of the letters in this group, something should be said about their authorship. Most, if not all, of the Pauline Epistles we have considered thus far may safely be assigned to Paul. But scholars have divided sharply over the question: "Who wrote the Pastorals?" Frequently we read a statement that takes it for granted that Paul is not the author. Again, others speak as though the authorship has never been a matter of dispute. Several reasons are given for doubting that Paul wrote them, at least in their present form, but we do not have the space to discuss this difficult subject. Until further light is thrown upon it, however, we shall continue to regard these letters as Pauline, and bearing the mark of his personality. See Dummelow's commentary for further discussion of authorship.

They contain instructions for the training and administration of churches and the proper treatment of church members, and the persons to whom they are addressed are mentioned in the letters.

I Timothy. Timothy probably became a Christian as a result of the preaching of Paul on his first missionary journey, when he visited Lystra in A.D. 47. He is described as already a disciple when first mentioned in the account of the second missionary journey in Acts. (16:1.) Timothy was a companion and assistant to Paul. He went with Paul on his last trip to Jerusalem and was with him in Rome during his imprisonment. He is associated with the Apostle in the Epistles to the Colossians and Philippians. At the time of the writing of this letter, probably between A.D. 64 and 66, Timothy was in charge of the church at Ephesus. It is generally thought to have been written after Paul had been released from his first imprisonment.

Paul's chief purpose in writing was to tell Timothy how to deal with the false teaching which threatened the church. He also sent instructions concerning the organization of the church and the kind of men to be chosen as presbyters and deacons. (Cf. Dummelow, page 995.) We may more readily understand the Epistle by regarding it as the "charge" of an older missionary of the cross to a young man who is to carry on the work the older man must soon lay down. It is possible to arrange the thought of this letter around the specific charges Paul makes to Timothy.

II Timothy. This is probably the last letter Paul wrote. He is believed to have been in prison at Rome for the second time. It would not be long before he would die for the faith as a martyr. We do not know what charges were brought against him at this time. In his loneliness and danger, he wrote to Timothy during the early part of A.D. 67 or 68. His purpose in writing was to encourage Timothy in his work as an evangelist and to urge him to come to Rome as soon as possible as a friend and helper. He also wanted to give Timothy further instructions about the affairs of the church, similar to those given in the first letter. It consists of expressions of affection, warnings, exhortations, and instructions.

Titus. Paul had left Titus in Crete to carry on the work there. It is not known when Titus began this work. He was a trusted companion of Paul and had served him faithfully in many instances.

The Epistle was most likely written after Paul's first imprisonment, about A.D. 65 or 66. It has a twofold purpose: to instruct his young helper in how to deal with false teaching in the churches, and in how to select the right kind of church officers. It is a highly personal letter but was no doubt intended for public reading in the churches, or at least Paul expected that the contents would be made known so as to give Titus the apostolic authority needed to handle a difficult situation

IX. THE EPISTLE TO THE HEBREWS AND THE GENERAL EPISTLES

1. *Hebrews*

Scholars have found the question of authorship of Hebrews a most baffling one. Their uncertainty at this point is evident from the various efforts to assign it first to one and then to another of the early Christians. Paul, Peter, Apollos, Barnabas, Silas, Philip, Luke, Aquila, and Priscilla—the names of all these are found in the modern guesses as to who wrote this Epistle.

The place of writing, date, and destination are equally matters of dispute and uncertainty. These questions cannot be answered until the authorship is determined. More recently, the view that it was written to Christians in Rome has gained favor among those who have devoted much time to studying Hebrews. Were the readers Jewish or Gentile Christians or is it written to both? This we do not know for certain. It was formerly thought that they were Jewish Christians who were being persuaded to turn back to Judaism, but many now hold the opinion that it was not written to prevent a return to Judaism but to warn against apostasy and sheer indifference on the part of the readers who were one-time pagans. This view would call for a later date. It would also relate the persecution and martyrdom referred to in the Epistle to the reign of Domitian, when Emperor worship was forced upon Christians. The date would probably be between A.D. 81 and 85.

The nature of this writing as an epistle calls for special comment. It ends like an epistle but does not begin like one. Was it, then, written primarily as an epistle, or was it a sermon prepared for oral delivery and later sent out as a letter? Its language shows more elegance and finish than that of any other book of the New Testament. Its author was a well-trained student and thinker, and his eloquence is more like that of a speaker than a writer. Yet the simplest solution is that it was a written homily which the author sent to a community whose members and needs he knew well.

The situation to which the writer addresses this masterly work is somewhat as follows: The readers were tempted to drift away from Christianity; there is a decided lack of the boldness and confidence and strong hope which marked the early Christian temper; they had become indifferent toward the fundamentals of the faith; they neglected the assembly; the expectation of Christ's return no longer played the part in their religious lives that it had in their fathers'; and persecution, which they had formerly known, was about to begin once again.

The enthusiasm they once felt for the gospel must be rekindled, their faith must be strengthened, and they must be encouraged for the fires of persecution which were rushing toward them. The author's theme is the complete and final chapter of the revelation made in Christ; that is, the superiority and finality of Christianity. His aim is to prove that what they possess is the absolute religion. He does this by contrasting Christianity and Judaism which alone, of all existing religions, could claim to have been given by God.

2. *The General Epistles*

As we have already seen, the letters which bear the names of James, Peter, John, and Jude have been grouped together and are known as the "Catholic" or "General" Epistles. This group of Epistles has been assigned to four different men. Two of them had grown up in the same home with Jesus and had known him intimately from childhood. Two others were with him from the early days of his ministry and had a part in establishing the church after his ascension. For discussion of the authorship of these Epistles see Dummelow's commentary.

One of the chief values of these Epistles is the splendid picture they give of the early Christian church, portraying its essential features from the early ministry of James to the last years of the Apostle John. We find historical references which carry us back to the ministry of Christ and the work of the Apostles. Some passages are obscure and difficult, but for the most part, the teachings are plain and contain principles which can be helpfully applied to the life and problems of the modern church.

James

Our interest in this Epistle is increased when we realize that it is probably the earliest of the New Testament letters, being assigned by many scholars to A.D. 45, or not long after. (See Dummelow.) Its author is believed to be James, the brother of our Lord and the head of the Jerusalem church. A considerable difference of opinion exists as to the readers James has in mind. Some think that he is addressing all Jews who were then scattered throughout the world. Others think that he is writing only to Jewish Christians outside Jerusalem. The latter view seems more in accord with the purpose and thought of the Epistle. It should be remembered that as the leader of the Christians in the Holy City, James would not have been regarded with favor by Jews anywhere who were not Christians.

The purpose of his writing was to reform and correct certain sins and errors which Jewish Christians were likely to follow, and to encourage them in the difficulties they faced as Christians. In order to clear up their confused notion about the nature of faith, James emphatically asserts that genuine faith begets good works, otherwise faith is dead. A close examination of the contents will give us a good idea of how the first generation of Jewish Christians looked upon Christianity, and the circumstances under which the new movement grew up.

I Peter

Much controversy has been carried on concerning the persons addressed in this letter. Peter opens by saluting "the strangers scattered throughout Pontus, Galatia, Cappadocia, Asia, and Bithynia." The question at issue is whether he is writing specifically to Jewish Christians or to the whole body of Christians, Jews and Gentiles, inhabiting the region comprised in modern Asia Minor. The term "dispersion," as we have seen, was carried over by James from the ancient people of God to the Christians. It seems obvious that the writer has in mind Gentile readers for the most part. (1:14; 2:9-10; 3:6; 4:3.) He is writing to churches Paul had founded and nurtured, and to which Paul had written other letters, such as Colossians and Ephesians.

Paul's letters to the Romans and Ephesians should be studied in connection with this Epistle. The date of First Peter is placed around A.D. 64 or 65. We do not know the place from which it was written.

Peter writes in a simple, striking, and forcible style. He makes many sudden and abrupt transitions in thought, perhaps the product of an impulsive character. The manner of presentation and the content of the Epistle are peculiar to the writer, but the doctrine set forth is the same as that found in Paul's Epistles. The grace of God and the Christians' hope for the future stand out as the two themes around which he centers his letter. It is obvious that his purpose in writing is to give encouragement to persecuted Christians. They are assured that they need have no fear because they are securely kept in the grace of God and have a crown of life awaiting them at the end.

II Peter

Serious doubt has been felt as to the authorship of II Peter. This has been true down through the centuries although there have been those in every generation of scholars who regarded it as the work of Peter. Doubt has existed because of the difference in style between it and First Peter, the latter being simpler in style and more facile in expression. Even Calvin felt some hesitancy about II Peter because of the "discrepancies between it and the First." Like Calvin, however, we may assign it to the Apostle until further light is thrown upon its authorship, for there is historical evidence which supports the view that it is a genuine product of the pen of Peter. If Peter did not write it, we need not attempt to conjecture who the writer may have been.

The readers, then, would be the same as those of the First Epistle.

Their circumstances, however, have changed and they are threatened with danger from within the churches rather than from without. False teachers are among them and deny Christ in doctrine and conduct. They especially ridicule the idea of the return of Christ. His long delay has led them to reject the possibility of his coming again at all. Their unbelief is expressed in immoral living. This Epistle was written to warn against such errors and to urge them to more exemplary living. Knowledge is the keynote of the letter, but the main subject with which the writer deals is the return of Christ. This Epistle should be studied in connection with the writing of Jude.

I John

The author of the Fourth Gospel is evidently the writer of this Epistle. The same general style and use of language are found in both. The Epistle takes it for granted that the readers are acquainted with the Gospel. Both were sent to the same churches. Many think that the Epistle was sent along with or not long after the Gospel. Thus questions of date, place, and purpose of writing this letter are closely linked with similar questions concerning the Fourth Gospel. The peculiar dangers to which it is specifically directed are two closely related developments of Gnosticism: a tendency to deny the reality of the Incarnation, and laxity in morals.

This Epistle has been called by some the "most controversial" of the New Testament writings. It is strongly polemic; but this should not cause us to lose sight of the main object of the letter, namely, to bring its readers into a genuine fellowship with God. Its purpose differs from that of the Gospel in that the Gospel was written to create faith and the Epistle to confirm the faith and develop the religious life of those who already believe.

It is not easy to follow the plan of the Epistle because the thought does not move from point to point in a straight line. It is more like a winding staircase—revolving around the same center, recurring to the same topics, but on a higher level. The mode of thinking is "spiral," and what we may call "cycles" of thought appear in the main divisions of the Epistle. Thus we can find certain fundamental ideas concerning the nature of God grouped around such watchwords as "God is light," "God is righteous," and "God is love." Three corresponding Christian graces are belief, righteousness, and love. These themes are introduced several times and are brought into every possible relation to one another, and are presented as "tests" in Christian experience.

II John

Almost every phrase in this Epistle occurs in I John. Because of this fact, it has sometimes been called a "miniature edition" of the larger work. Tradition has assigned it to the Apostle John, although much speculation has taken place as to whether the "presbyter" or "elder" is to be identified with "the disciple whom Jesus loved." We do not know the date or exact circumstances of the writing of this small letter.

We are unable to decide with any degree of certainty to whom the Epistle is addressed. The "elect lady" of verse one has been taken by some to refer to a particular church. Others regard the recipient as an individual.

The purpose of the writer is twofold: to warn against the same false doctrines dealt with in I John, and to urge the reader not to extend hospitality to teachers of such views. He regards them as enemies to the church. Hospitality was looked upon not only as a Christian grace, but as a means of spreading the gospel. When abused by false teachers it could help destroy the faith. When courtesy and hospitality were given to teachers of error, support might be afforded to their evil cause. False teachers are not to be entertained when in doing so truth is endangered.

III John

Here we get an intimate glimpse of some aspects of the life of the early church in Asia Minor toward the close of the first century. We are given pen portraits of three church members from the Apostolic Age, and an insight into the administration of the church at this period. It would seem that the writer is charged with the supervision of several churches; this is one of them. He had sent some evangelists to the various churches with proper credentials. When they came to the church of which Gaius and Diotrephes were members, Gaius had welcomed and entertained them, but Diotrephes, who seems to have possessed some local authority, refused them admittance to the church and hospitality. He threatened to excommunicate those who did receive them. When the rejected teachers returned to Ephesus they testified to the church there of the courage and generosity of Gaius, and of the conceit, love of power, arrogance, and tyranny of Diotrephes. The teachers were apparently sent forth again with Demetrius, who carries this letter of commendation to Gaius and of warning to Diotrephes. A similar letter was written to the church, but was not effective in overcoming the opposition of the vain Diotrephes.

This letter is not concerned with heresy. The situation is in a sense the reverse of that in the church to which II John is written. Then the writer was concerned because false teachers were being received and given an opportunity to teach error. Here he is disturbed because accredited teachers are refused an opportunity to teach. There is no intimation of heresy on the part of Diotrephes, or indication that Gaius is a defender of the faith. It seems to be a question of the abuse of authority.

The Epistle of Jude

The writer of this Epistle was probably one of the four brethren of the Lord, and a brother of the author of the Epistle of James. If so we have two New Testament books by members of Jesus' own family. We know nothing of Jude other than the fact that he did not believe in Christ until after the resurrection. (John 7:5; Acts 1:14.)

Jude and II Peter are closely related in thought and form. Some think that one writer uses much of the other's work, but they do not know which was written first. Those who think that Jude was written first place the time of writing before A.D. 66. Students who regard II Peter as the older place the date of Jude between A.D. 70 and 81.

We do not know who the readers were. The Epistle seems intended for a special occasion and perhaps was addressed to a particular church. The readers must have been Jewish Christians, for it takes for granted a certain knowledge of Jewish religious writings which would not have been familiar to Gentiles. It may have been intended for Jewish Christians of Palestine, but its destination must remain pure conjecture. The writer has learned that false teaching has "crept" into the church or churches he has in view. He is disturbed by this report and writes to warn them against it and to describe the punishment the offenders will receive. He does not define the errors but assumes that his readers understand what he has in mind. The aim of Jude is purely practical. Again, we see that form of Gnosticism which denied Christ and led to immoral practices. This error seems to have been influential in the Christian community and must have been a serious threat to Christianity.

X. THE REVELATION

1. *Title*

The proper title of this book is "The Revelation of Jesus Christ." The writer speaks of it as a "Revelation" or "Apocalypse." The name "Revelation" is given to it because it is the disclosure of "things which must shortly come to pass." The word "Apocalypse" means an "unveiling" or "uncovering" of something which has been hidden or covered up. As used by the author of Revelation, it means to disclose to the mind truth otherwise or hitherto unknown. He intends to make known something about Christ and his church that had not been revealed before.

2. *Form*

The apocalyptic form serves to explain the symbolism and doctrine of last things in Revelation. We should guard against a very common error in thinking of apocalyptic literature, namely, that the term "apoclyptic" should be applied to any passage of Scripture which deals with what is to take place at the end of time. The word used for this latter doctrine is "eschatology." Often it is taken for granted that the discourse of Jesus in the thirteenth chapter of the Gospel according to Mark is apocalyptic. It is often called the "Little Apocalypse" simply because the writer is prophesying of future events. This is also true of Paul's references to the Second Coming of Christ in I Thessalonians 4:13-18 and II Thessalonians 2:1-10. In fact, neither one of these descriptions of the end is "apocalyptic," but all are eschatalogical. In short, the two terms are not identical and should not be so used. Some scholars think that Jesus was even "anti-apocalyptical," because apocalyptic literature was usually characterized by materialism, literalism, and defective spiritual attitude toward God, and by a limited ethical view toward man. This helps to account for the fact that so few of the many apocalypses written were given a place in the canon of Scripture. Naturally, there would be varying degrees of merit in such writings, and Revelation stands at the top.

3. Destination

Revelation is addressed to the seven churches of the Roman province of Asia: Ephesus, Smyrna, Pergamos, Thyatira, Sardis, Philadelphia, and Laodicea. Seven was regarded as a sacred number, signifying completeness. It is thought that it was used here to indicate that the book was really addressed to the whole church.

4. Author

The author was a Jewish Christian. He calls himself "John." (1:1, 4, 9; 21:2; 22:8.) No other explanation or description is given. Early Christian tradition holds that the Apostle John wrote it. He was acquainted with the churches of the Roman province of Asia, and was in exile in Patmos. This tradition persists in the Christian church despite the differences between Revelation and the other writings of the New Testament which are assigned to this apostle. Again we are dealing with a debatable question, and opinion differs widely. For a fuller discussion of authorship see the Westminster Bible dictionary and Dummelow's commentary.

5. Date

As to the date of Revelation, two principal opinions have been held. One assigns it to the period of the Neronian persecution, just prior to A.D. 70 and the fall of Jerusalem. The other, to which most subscribe, places it in the reign of Domitian, about A.D. 94-96. This view is in keeping with early tradition which held that it was written toward the close of his reign, A.D. 95 or 96.

6. *Occasion and Purpose*

The book was called forth by the terrible situation which existed in the church due to the attempt to make the worship of Caesar obligatory throughout Asia Minor. The Christians had refused to submit to this practice. Because of their refusal persecution had overtaken them. John was exiled on the island of Patmos. Danger was imminent for all Christians.

He writes to encourage them to faith and fortitude. He does this in a series of letters and then proceeds to show them why they can afford to hold out patiently. Their suffering will not last long, the last days are upon them, and the triumph of Christ and his cause is near. It is not a book of doom or despair, as is often supposed, but a summons to faith and courage. The real note of the book is one of exaltation—approaching victory should steel them for impending suffering. Its theme is to warn and fortify by showing that God will most certainly act very soon in this hour of final crisis.

7. *Contents*

Many people find Revelation a difficult and mysterious writing. Consequently the average reader is acquainted only with small portions—those that are not couched in symbolic language and fantastic imagery. The author intended, however, that his work should be read aloud, probably in the churches, and expected the hearers to understand. He did not believe that he was writing something to intrigue and confuse. His readers were no doubt well acquainted with apocalyptic imagery and symbols and possessed what we may call a "key" to understanding what appears to us beyond apprehension. Recent studies in contemporary literature of this sort have made this clear, and have also provided us with the means of getting behind most of the symbols to his real meaning. But we may never be able to fit all of his sayings together so as to feel certain that we can reconstruct his thought and meaning accurately.

There seem to be a few basic assumptions underlying the entire plan and structure of this book: (1) The coming of the Lord was close at hand; it would take place soon. (2) His coming would be preceded by a series of unusual events of a disastrous nature. (3) Immediately before the Messiah appeared an "Antichrist" would arise in whom the forces of evil would be incarnated and who would represent Satan himself in the final struggle. (4) The heavenly city, the new Jerusalem, would take the place of the present earthly one— which had already been destroyed—and would be the abode of the redeemed people of God.

8. *Interpretation*

Revelation is not an easy book to understand, for the average reader or even the Bible student. It should be borne in mind that while this book was to reveal to those who could get the meaning of the symbols and imagery of the author it was intended to conceal the meaning from those who stood on the outside.

Few, if any, real scholars have ever claimed to be able to give an exhaustive and full explanation to this book. Calvin did not even undertake to write a commentary on it, and most students of Scripture have spoken upon it with caution and humility. A fairly sound principal to follow is to try to find out the various views about Revelation but to deal with caution with those writers who are sure that they have said the last word as to what it means. Several types of interpretation have been given to it.

Futurist

One view regards it as a predictive description of the events that shall immediately precede the end of the age. Chapters 1—3 are exempted from this method of interpretation.

Preterist

The Preterist method of interpretation is exactly opposite from the Futurist. It holds that the author is concerned solely with his own times, speaking only to men and conditions then existing. He regards his own generation as the last upon earth, and holds that the end of the age is near. All of the symbolism of the book applies to events and personages of the first century. Its chief interest to us is literary and historical. It was of real value only to the author and his contemporaries.

Continuous-Historical

The third view, known as the Continuous-Historical, escapes the one-sidedness of both of the preceding. It holds that the author's vision does portray things that are to happen at the end of this world, but that it also includes the whole interval between his own day and the end. Those who belong to this school of thought see in the visions of Revelation a successive portrayal of the events of Christian history and attempt to identify its symbolism with such historical events as the growth of Islam, the Papacy, the Reformation, and countless others.

All three of these views have proved unsatisfactory because of the effort to identify the contents of the visions with external events of some particular period or periods of history.

Symbolic

The term symbolic is given to a fourth way of explaining Revelation. It regards the visions as figurative presentations of certain truths or principles which shall exist throughout the church. It finds here the great principles of the conflict between good and evil, of the growing struggle between them, and of the final victory of the good. It does not take literally the mathematical numbers and symbols of Revelation. These are thought to disclose the principles of God's government of the church and world, and are common to every age of history. They are timeless.

Recurrent Prophetic

Still another method has been used more recently, since the rediscovery of the true nature of apocalyptic literature. It has been designated the Recurrent Prophetic method. According to this view, Revelation was written primarily to meet a present need of its time, and was designed to be understood by the men of that generation who understood and used apocalyptic language. Its references are largely to the affairs of the author's time, but the task he was trying to perform determined the peculiar meanings of his language. The book is addressed to a need which arises often, and the same principles can always be applied to similar circumstances. Thus the events dealt with in Revelation were imminent but they have a permanent interest. This will continue down to the end of time. In the book of Revelation we are privileged to take a glance at the whole course of the church's experience. The writer saw eternal forces at work in the affairs of his time, and regarded them as the underlying spiritual realities of the whole course of time, whether the end be near or remote.

While many find these two latter views more satisfactory than the others, it cannot be said that they have answered all the problems which arise in the interpretation of Revelation.

Perhaps we cannot do better than to close this discussion by giving the opinion of the Muratorian Canon, dated in the second century, as pointing us to the right way of reading this book. It says, "John, too, in the Apocalypse, although he writes only to seven churches yet addresses all."

THE FOUR GOSPELS

MATTHEW through JOHN

JOSEPH M. GARRISON

THE FOUR GOSPELS

THE FOUR GOSPELS

THE LIFE OF JESUS

A Survey Course in the Four Gospels

Each of the four Gospels is unique. Authorship, style, language, order, and materials are all different. They are one, however, in purpose. They were written to provide a record and an interpretation of the life and work of Jesus. In his life and work we find the clue to the fine and full life for all mankind.

The Gospels were written some thirty to seventy years after the crucifixion of Jesus. While Jesus walked among men there was little felt need for written records of his life. Experiences and memories were too vivid for that. As a new generation appeared, and as the story of Jesus' life spread among strangers, the need for the Gospels became very real. Mark is the earliest of the four records in the New Testament. Luke and Matthew come next. John was the last to be written.

The Gospel writers undertook to answer the natural and normal questions anyone would ask in trying to become acquainted with Jesus. When and where was he born, and under what circumstances? Who were his parents? What characterized his childhood and youth? What was the nature of his life work? What did he think about God and man? How did he regard the Jews of his day? What was his attitude toward the Jewish moral code and the religious rituals which were rooted back in the long history of his people? What was his attitude toward the Gentile world in general and Roman rulers in particular? How was he received by those who knew him? What were the major aspects of his life and work? How long did he live? What was the outcome of his life? What is the meaning of Jesus' life and work for humanity?

Our primary aim is to ask these natural questions which are asked in each new generation, and to seek the answers from the four Gospels. For our purpose we are limiting our sources to the four Gospels,

Davis and Gehman's Westminster Bible dictionary and Dummelow's one volume commentary. Those seeking a more detailed study will want to refer to other helpful reference books.

In general there are two ways to study the life of Jesus. The first is to follow chronologically the events in his life. The other is to single out the central ideas and follow them as they unfold and develop through the Gospels. Our method will be a combination of both of these approaches. We will follow the broad stream of Jesus' life, and as central ideas are introduced we will try to trace them in their development throughout the life of Jesus.

When we adopt this combined procedure our study shapes up into twelve divisions. In studying each of the twelve divisions we shall endeavor to take three steps. First there will be a brief narrative of the events in the life of Jesus up to a certain stage. These events usually introduce or cluster around a central idea and have outreach throughout his life. Some effort will be made to follow through on the central idea involved. This will be followed by a list of what appear to be the more important questions involved. The final stage will be a citation of specific and general study references in the Gospels, in the Bible dictionary, and in the commentary.

I. JESUS' BIRTH AND CHILDHOOD

"Thou shalt call his name JESUS; for it is he that shall save his people from their sins."—Matthew 1:21.

John 1:1-18
Luke 1:1—2:52; 3:23-38
Matthew 1:1—2:23

Thrilling circumstances surround the birth and youth of Jesus. They have been told and retold with new wonder in each new generation.

The story opens with God dealing in an unmistakable way with two families. One family would be given a son long after their age of bearing children; his name was to be John. He would be filled with the Holy Spirit from his birth and he would prepare the way of the Lord—the promised and long-awaited Messiah. The other family would be given a son of the Holy Spirit and his name was to be

Jesus. He would be the promised Saviour, the Son of David, the Son of Abraham.

Both families believed the long-standing promises which God had given to Abraham. But, more than that, they believed the specific promises which God had given to them.

Jesus was born of humble parentage in a borrowed stable. He was at once the object of wonder and hatred, of hope and fear. To ensure his safekeeping his mother and Joseph were led of God to flee into Egypt. When they thought all danger had passed they started their return to Bethlehem. They were led of God to set up their home in Nazareth. Here Jesus spent his early youth. At twelve, he caused amazement by his announcement that he must be about his Father's business. Then for eighteen years he grew in wisdom and in stature, and in favor with God and man.

With these quick strides we cover thirty of the thirty-three years of Jesus' life. We see promises given of God and fulfilled of God. We see human agents worthy to be used miraculously of God. We see the manifest appearance of the hand of God in small matters and in great matters. We see the real humanity of Jesus. We see the completeness of his divine origin.

The events connected with the early life of Jesus suggest a number of questions:

Who were Zacharias and his wife and just how were they to share in the coming of Christ?

Luke 1:5-25, 57-80.

How was the birth of Jesus related to the religious history of Israel?

Dummelow: "The Messianic Hope" (pp. xlv-xlvii); 'The Book of the Generation" (p. 623); "The Christian Doctrine of the Incarnation" (p. cvi); "The Magnificat" (pp. 739-740).

What kind of people were Mary and Joseph?

Luke 1:26-56; 2:1-7. Dummelow: "The Annunciation" (pp. 738-739); "The Incarnation and the Virgin Birth" (pp. 624-625); "A Just Man" (p. 625); Westminster Bible dictionary: articles on Joseph (p. 330) and Mary the Virgin (pp. 380-381).

What groups of people bore witness to the fact of Jesus' birth?

Luke 2:8-20, 22-39; Matthew 2:1-12, 13-23.

What did the early worshipers see in this ("supposed") carpenter's Son?

Dummelow: "Announcement to the Shepherds" (p. 742); "The Wise Men" (pp. 626-628); "Simeon and the Nunc Dimittis" (pp. 742-743); "Anna the Prophetess" (p. 743).

How early and to what extent did Jesus feel that he was the Son of God?

Luke 2:41-52.

What part did Joseph and Mary have in the training of Jesus?

Luke 2:19-24, 40-52. Dummelow: "Childhood and Youth of Jesus" (pp. lxxiv-lxxv).

Enumerate the evidences we have that the hand of God was showing itself in the birth and youth of Jesus.

General References

"The Gospels in General," Dummelow (p. 617).

General Characteristics and Analysis of Matthew, Dummelow (p. 620ff.).

General Characteristics and Analysis of Mark, Dummelow (p. 723ff.).

General Characteristics and Analysis of Luke, Dummelow (p. 735ff.).

General Characteristics and Analysis of John, Dummelow (p. 770ff.).

Article on Bethlehem, in Westminster Bible dictionary (pp. 69-70).

Article on Nazareth, in Westminster Bible dictionary (p. 419).

II. Jesus' Way Prepared

"Make ye ready the way of the Lord."—Mark 1:3.

Mark 1:1-13
Luke 3:1—4:13
Matthew 3:1—4:11

John, the son of Zacharias, grew up and became a preacher. He spoke of himself as the forerunner of one who would come after him who would be the greater. The central theme of his preaching was a call to repentance. This was the essential step toward preparing for a new order. To a very large extent he was successful. All kinds of people joined his movement, and others began to ask questions. The repentance which John called for was a complete change of outlook and conduct toward God and his purpose for men. This was the only way men could share in what God was about to give to the world through the coming of the Messiah. This is what may be called the immediate preparation of Jesus' way by John.

There were at least two other kinds of preparation which entered the picture. The first was the long-term preparation of the nation of which John was a part. This takes us back through the Old Testament story of God's dealing with Israel. Through the generations since Abraham there had been a degree of preparation moving to this hour. But for four centuries, from the time of the prophet Malachi, things had moved slowly but surely toward a "fulness of the time."

These four centuries brought many changes among the Jews. Each change contributed in some way to the humbling of a people for the coming of a gracious Saviour. Political life looked bad. Rome's heavy heel was keenly felt by the Jews. They had been able to do little but submit. Religious life among the Jews had become largely a matter of forms, rituals, ceremonies, and other externals. Several religious parties—the scribes, Pharisees, Sadducees—and the Herodians, sought to manipulate the common people and competed with one another over vested interests. There was general unrest among common people over the state of religion.

All in all, the Jews saw no hope except as God might strike down their enemies and set up a new order which they thought of as a Super-Roman Kingdom. Against such a background the possibility of the coming of the Messiah was "good news."

Another aspect of the preparation for Jesus' ministry was his own personal preparation. This is pictured for us in his lining up with the movement of repentance which John initiated, and in his baptism and his temptation. At the heart of the temptation stands a question Jesus had to answer, "Was he the Son of God?" To him the issue was clear, there was to be no testing of the extent of that relationship.

He must accept it in faith and move forward with it in faith, no matter where it might lead.

These three aspects of the preparation for Jesus' ministry lead to these questions:

How was the way of the coming one to be prepared, as John saw it?

Luke 3:1-14; Mark 1:1-8.

What did the people see in John the Baptizer?

Luke 3:7-18.

What is the meaning of repentance as preached by John, and later by Jesus?

Dummelow: "John the Baptist's Ministry" (pp. 629-630).

To what extent did the Jews feel the need for a Saviour given of God?

What kind of Saviour were the Jews anticipating?

See articles on the Messiah (p. 393) and on Christ (p. 100) in Westminster Bible dictionary.

Why did Jesus seek baptism of John?

Matthew 3:13-17. Dummelow: "Baptism of Jesus" (pp. 631-632); "The Baptism" (p. lxxv).

How did Jesus show his complete trust in God?

Matthew 4:1-11. Article, "The Temptation," in Westminster Bible dictionary (p. 305).

What respect for people did Jesus show in his refusal of the offers of the Devil?

Matthew 4:1-11. Dummelow: "The Temptation" (pp. 632-633).

What kind of kingdom did Jesus evidence that he would pursue?

Matthew 4:1-11. Dummelow: "The Temptation" (p. lxxv).

What kind of Messiah did John bear witness to?

Luke 3:15-17; John 1:29-34.

General References

Concerning the Roman rule, see article, "Rome," in Westminster Bible dictionary (pp. 519-520).

Concerning the several religious parties, see "Scribe" (p. 539); "Pharisees" (p. 476); "Sadducees" (p. 524).

III. JESUS' FIELD OF WORK

"And Jesus went about in all Galilee . . . And the report of him went forth into all Syria."—Matthew 4:23-24.

John 1:35—4:54

Jesus' field of work changed from time to time in very close relation to the Passover seasons and the changes that became necessary as the events of his life moved forward through three years toward his crucifixion.

The recorded details of Jesus' life between his temptation and his entry upon his public ministry are few. He attended a wedding at Cana in Galilee where his first miracle was wrought—the changing of water into wine. Then he made a short visit to Capernaum. This brings us up to the first of four Passover seasons to occur during his public ministry. Some think there were only three Passovers during Jesus' ministry. It is on the basis of the Passover seasons that it is calculated that Jesus' ministry covered about three years.

With the approach of the first Passover season Jesus went up to Jerusalem. On this visit to Jerusalem, he drove the money-changers from the Temple* and in a sense began to offer himself to people generally. Immediately he met hostile opposition. A few people like Nicodemus seem to have been favorably impressed.

On leaving Jerusalem Jesus traveled around in the Judean country for a period estimated at about nine months. He worked in rather close association with John the Baptist. John was growing unpopular with the political leaders, which resulted in his imprisonment and finally his death. When John was imprisoned, Jesus moved into Galilee where he labored until the time of the second Passover. Again he went to Jerusalem for the celebration.

When Jesus left Jerusalem he returned to Galilee where he continued to concentrate his work for what seems to be another whole year. It was a period of public favor, crowded with cures and teachings. A conflict with the rulers was beginning to be evident, but over

---

* The Synoptic Gospels place the cleasing of the Temple at the end of Jesus' ministry. On the possibility of two cleansings see Dummelow, p. 694.

against this there was much favor among the common people, who heard him gladly.

When the third year of Jesus' ministry opens, following the third Passover, which apparently he did not attend in Jerusalem, we find Jesus still in the region of Galilee.

In the early part of the third year of Jesus' work there was marked change in his ministry. He turned to a plan of spending his time largely with the disciples. His primary purpose seems to have been that of preparing his disciples for his crucifixion.

During the last half of the third year he moved into the region of Perea. Since this was near Jerusalem, he attended the Jewish feasts. Each time, opposition gathered, so that for the most part Jesus chose to withdraw almost entirely from the multitudes into an intimate association with the disciples and a few chosen friends.

His final entry into Jerusalem was during the last Passover season to occur during his ministry. At this time he was tried and crucified.

In the face of these numerous changes in the field of Jesus' ministry, a number of questions appear:

Where did Jesus begin his ministry?

John 3:22-36. See Dummelow (p. 780), comment on verses 22-36.

Why did Jesus turn to Galilee for his major field of work?

Mark 1:14-15; Luke 4:14-32; John 4:1-3. See Dummelow (p. 634), comment on verse 12.

Locate the Passover seasons mentioned in the Gospels during the public ministry of Jesus.

John 2:13—3:21; John 5:1-47; John 6:22-71; Matthew 26:1-29. See chart, "Harmony of the Four Gospels," in Westminster Bible dictionary (pp. 211-216).

What were the major changes in Jesus' ministry which can be identified with each of the three years of Jesus' public work?

See "Harmony of the Four Gospels" in Westminster Bible dictionary (pp. 211-216) for a detailed listing of the events in the life of Jesus. Get a general view of the major events in his life with reference to the field in which he worked. See Dummelow, "Sketch of the Ministry" (pp. lxxvi-lxxviii), for a running narrative of the major changes in the field of Jesus' ministry, and some of the factors causing him to move around. Dummelow uses three Passover seasons.

What was the significance of the Passover for the Jews?

See "Passover," in Westminster Bible dictionary (pp. 452-453). To what extent did Jesus use circumstances to discover God's will for the general direction of his life and work?

John 4:1-42. Dummelow: "Christ in Samaria" (p. 781). John 6:15-21; 7:1-9.

General References

Study the map, "Palestine During the Ministry of Jesus," in Westminster Bible dictionary (Plate XIV). Locate on it Judea, Galilee, Perea, Nazareth, Capernaum, Jerusalem, Bethany, and Sea of Galilee. See Westminster Bible dictionary for articles on any of the above places.

IV. JESUS' MANY MIRACLES

"And he healed many that were sick with divers diseases, and cast out many demons."—Mark 1:34.

Matthew 4:12-17; 8:2—9:13; 12:1-30
Mark 1:14—3:12
Luke 4:14—6:16

The imprisonment of John marks the end of Jesus' ministry in Judea, the southern area of Palestine. Jesus moved north into Galilee, which was the scene of more than half of his ministry. Jesus' movement into Galilee marks the beginning of his public works.

One of the first places Jesus visited in Galilee was Nazareth. He was rejected by his own people so he moved on to Capernaum. Immediately his fame, for good works, began to spread abroad. The miracle in Cana of Galilee several months before proved to be but the beginning of many good and mighty works. During the early part of this Galilean ministry, perhaps for as much as a year, the Gospel writers indicate that Jesus wrought many miracles. A number of them are reported in detail. In addition there were many others. Quite often the Gospel writers generalize, saying that Jesus "went about in all Galilee . . . healing all manner of disease and all manner of sickness among the people." (Matt. 4:23.)

One of the central facts in this period of Jesus' life is his mighty works of healing. This phase of Jesus' work is designated by several different names such as miracles, wonders, signs, and mighty works of God. It was all of these, and more.

Several general observations are important as we look at Jesus' miracles as a whole. Usually there was a very large benevolent side to the use Jesus made of his miraculous power. For example, some person in dire need was cured. But beyond that there were other benevolent qualities in such works. The very acts of healing were often done in the most benevolent way, such as going into the home of Jairus or touching the leper. Usually the news spread and others believed or sought the help of Jesus.

Finally, through these works, some aspect of Jesus' character was revealed. In John's Gospel this is emphasized in particular. John uses the incidents of healing without regard to chronological order, as illustrations of the nature of Jesus' life and mission. The revelation of Jesus' character through his good works seems to be progressive and moves to the manifestation of more and more power.

The customs and ceremonies of the day have considerable bearing on the account of the miracles in the Gospels, and the way in which Jesus went about an act of healing. Often the steps toward a cure involved the use of some of the customs of the day, as when those cured of leprosy had to show themselves to the priest in the Temple for purification. Sometimes the healing cut across some custom or ceremony and became the occasion for men to begin to criticize Jesus.

The disciples were present for most of the healings. As observers they learned much. It is important to keep in mind the effect of these works on the disciples as a part of their preparation. In Jesus' works he often demonstrated his words. Quite often Jesus moved from a miracle to a teaching situation where he unfolded some aspect of the Kingdom.

The prominence of faith in the case of those cured is very important. Jesus was always looking for this and calling attention to its presence or lack of it.

Over against these observations a number of questions arise:
What do we mean by a miracle?

See article, "Miracle," in Westminster Bible dictionary (p. 399).
Dummelow: "Miracle" (pp. cxv-cxxii).

What did Jesus say about his use of miracles?

John 5:10-29.

How did the witness of miracles serve as a part of the training of the disciples?

Matthew 8:23-27.

What did the multitudes see in the miracle work of Jesus?

See articles, Demoniac (p. 136), Leprosy (pp. 355-356), Blindness (p. 77), in Westminster Bible dictionary.

Why did Jesus look for and honor faith in connection with healings?

What kind of faith was it?

Matthew 8:10; 9:2; 9:22; 9:29; 15:28; Mark 2:5; 5:34; 10:52; Luke 5:20; 7:9; 7:50; 8:48; 17:19.

See article on Faith in Westminster Bible dictionary (p. 180).

Why did Sabbath healings offend the Jews?

Matthew 12:1-14; Mark 3:1-6; Luke 6:1-11; John 5:1-18; 9:13-16.
See article on the Sabbath in Westminster Bible dictionary (pp. 521-523).
See comments in Dummelow (pp. 666-667).

What did the miracles reveal about the character of Jesus?

See the list of miracles for references.

What are the Gospel writers telling us about Jesus in the record of his miracles?

General References

Select seven different miracles for careful study. See Dummelow for comments on the miracles under the Scripture references. For the sake of a complete reference list, all of the 35 specific miracles are listed.

The Miracles of Jesus

	MATT.	MARK	LUKE	JOHN
1. Water to wine				2:1-11
2. Nobleman's son healed				4:46-54
3. Unclean spirit cast out of a man		1:21-28	4:31-37	
4. Simon's mother-in-law healed	8:14-17	1:29-34	4:38-41	
5. First net of fishes			5:1-11	
6. A leper healed	8:2-4	1:40-45	5:12-16	
7. Man sick of palsy healed	9:1-8	2:1-12	5:17-26	
8. Sabbath healing of impotent man				5:1-47
9. Sabbath healing of withered hand	12:9-14	3:1-6	6:6-11	
10. Centurion's servant healed	8:5-13		7:1-10	
11. Widow's son raised			7:11-17	
12. Sea made calm	8:23-27	4:35-41	8:22-25	
13. Demons cast out of two men	8:28-34	5:1-20	8:26-39	
14. Jarius' daughter raised	9:18-26	5:21-43	8:40-56	
15. Woman healed of issue of blood	9:18-26	5:21-43	8:40-56	
16. Two blind men healed	9:27-31			
17. A dumb man healed	9:32-34			
18. Blind and dumb man healed	12:22-37			
19. Five thousand fed	14:13-21	6:30-44	9:10-17	6:1-14
20. Jesus walks on the sea	14:22-33	6:47-53		6:16-21
21. Phoenician woman's daughter	15:21-28	7:24-30		
22. Deaf and dumb man healed		7:31-37		
23. Four thousand fed	15:32-39	8:1-9		
24. Blind man healed		8:22-26		
25. Boy healed of epilepsy	17:14-21	9:14-29	9:37-43	
26. Money from fish's mouth	17:24-27			
27. Man born blind healed				9:1-41
28. Woman's 18-year-old infirmity healed			13:10-17	
29. Man healed of dropsy			14:1-6	
30. Lazarus raised				11:1-44
31. Ten lepers healed-cleansed			17:11-19	
32. Bartimaeus receives sight	20:29-34	10:46-52	18:35-43	

	MATT.	MARK	LUKE	JOHN
33. Fig tree withers away	21:18-19	11:12-14, 20-25		
34. Malchus' ear restored			22:50-51	
35. Net filled with great fishes				21:1-14

V. JESUS' USE OF PARABLES IN TEACHING

"And with many such parables spake he the word unto them, as they were able to hear it."—Mark 4:33.

Matthew 8:5—13:58 (5:1—8:1)
Mark 3:13—6:6
Luke 6:17—8:56

The year and a half Jesus spent in Galilee was also characterized by much teaching. Beginning with the selection of the twelve apostles the record of Jesus' teaching becomes more prominent. During this period we find the Sermon on the Mount and the first group of parables. These are examples of the Master Teacher at work.

We know very little of the teaching of Jesus during the first year of his ministry; no doubt it was considerable. The healing ministry was the first to catch the public eye and to attract the multitudes to him. For Jesus, however, teaching seems to have had a larger place than healing.

Our introduction to Jesus as a teacher is in face-to-face relationships with individual learners. Probably much of his teaching was to individuals such as Nicodemus and the woman of Samaria. Certain parts of his teaching were for the multitudes generally. Other parts were for the official religious leaders. Still others were for his disciples. The audiences Jesus addressed had much to do with his method at a given time.

Two significant things about the teachings of Jesus stand out: (1) his subject matter, and (2) his method. In order to get at the subject matter we have to understand his method. Our study of his method ought, therefore, to precede a study of his content.

Jesus' method as a teacher had at least four major characteristics.

1. It was patterned after Oriental form in contrast to our Western form. The Oriental form is characterized by numerous sayings con-

cise in form yet conducive to long reflection, in contrast to an orderly discourse that begins with a subject and ends with a specific statement of practical application. There was also the possibility of wide variation in the matter of interpretation; one would see one thing, and another would see something else. This method was important since Jesus had to depend on the memory of his listeners, and since he frequently spoke to people who were trying to catch him up in his speech.

2. Most of the frequent and varied figures of speech which Jesus used were drawn from everyday life. These parabolic statements were designed to reveal and conceal the truth in his teaching. As opposition increased he made a larger use of parables.

3. The most characteristic method of Jesus' teaching was his use of parables. Something like a third of all Jesus' recorded teaching is in this form. Several principles are helpful in trying to understand Jesus' use of parables as a method of teaching.

(a) It is often helpful to let the characters in the parables be real and alive.

(b) Usually there is a larger setting which furnishes a good clue to the central emphasis in the parable.

(c) There is a central truth in each parable, which is often accented by numerous details; such details, while important, should be recognized as secondary.

(d) In a few instances Jesus made an application of the truth he was unfolding in a parable, but for the most part his hearers were left to make their own application.

(e) The central truth in each parable, while having some relation to the immediate situation, is also a timeless truth.

4. The written record of Jesus' teaching, as in the case of any written record, does not show the full personality of the teacher. Facial expressions and gestures cannot be written down. As a part of Jesus' method, he made use of a number of qualities of personality which are mentioned in the Gospels.

This general survey of Jesus' use of the parable as a method of teaching introduces a number of questions:

What is a parable?

See "Parable" in Westminster Bible dictionary (pp. 449-450).
Why did Jesus use parables so much? In the latter part of his
ministry why did these increase?

Mark 4:10-12; 4:33-34; Matthew 11:15-19; Matthew 13:10-17;
Luke 8:9-10.

How do we go about getting the meaning of a parable?

Note the principles listed above and apply them to several parables. For *interpretation* of specific parables see Dummelow, the
Scripture reference for the parable being studied.

What personal qualities make up a part of Jesus' method and
power as a teacher?

Matthew 7:29; John 7:26; Luke 4:32; Matthew 15:32.

What type of hearers did Jesus face as a teacher?

Mark 4:2-9, 10-20; Luke 8:4-8, 9-18.

What type of situations did Jesus use for teaching?

Matthew 13:1-3; 18:1-3; 19:27—20:16; 21:23-27; Luke 14:1-6, 25-
35; 15:1-3; 16:1; 18:1; 20:1-8.

Do the central truths of the parables have meaning for today?

Throughout this section our primary emphasis has been on the
parables in Jesus' teaching. Our emphasis has been on method, in contrast to content. A full list of the parables is included for general reference. The references given include the setting. Select five parables for
careful study of method.

The Major Parables of Jesus

	MATT.	MARK	LUKE	JOHN
1. Two Debtors			7:36-50	
2. The Sower	13:3-23	4:2-20	8:4-15	
3. Seed Growing Secretly		4:26-29		
4. The Tares	13:24-30			
5. The Mustard Seed	13:31-32	4:30-32	13:18-19	
6. The Leaven	13:33		13:20-21	
7. Hidden Treasure	13:44			
8. The Pearl of Great Price	13:45-46			
9. The Net	13:47-50			
10. The Unmerciful Servant	18:23-35			
11. The Good Samaritan			10:25-37	

	MATT.	MARK	LUKE	JOHN
12. The Friend at Midnight			11:5-13	
13. The Rich Fool			12:16-21	
14. The Fig Tree			13:1-9	
15. The Great Supper			14:15-24	
16. The Lost Sheep	18:12-14		15:1-7	
17. The Lost Coin			15:8-10	
18. The Lost Son			15:11-32	
19. The Unrighteous Steward			16:1-13	
20. The Rich Man and Lazarus			16:19-31	
21. Unprofitable Servants			17:7-10	
22. The Unjust Judge			18:1-8	
23. The Pharisee and Publican			18:9-14	
24. Laborers in the Vineyard	20:1-16			
25. The Pounds			19:11-27	
26. The Two Sons	21:28-32			
27. The Wicked Husbandmen	21:33-41	12:1-9	20:9-16	
28. The Rejected Stone	21:42-46	12:10-11	20:17-19	
29. The Marriage Feast	22:1-14			
30. The Ten Virgins	25:1-13			
31. The Talents	25:14-30			

The Parabolic Statements

	MATT.	MARK	LUKE	JOHN
1. Sign of the Temple				2:13-22
2. The Physician			4:16-37	
3. Bridegroom, Patches, Old Skins	9:14-17	2:18-22	5:33-39	
4. Blind Guiding, Mote and Beam	7:1-5		6:37-42	
5. Wise and Foolish Builders	7:24-27		6:46-49	
6. Children in the Market	11:16-19		7:31-35	
7. Satan's Kingdom	12:22-37	3:22-30		
8. Unclean Spirit	12:38-45			
9. The Householder	13:51-52			
10. Corban, Things That Defile	15:1-20	7:1-23		
11. Good Shepherd				10:1-21
12. Waiting Servants			12:35-40	
13. Wise Steward			12:42-48	
14. Seats at the Feast			14:7-11	

	MATT.	MARK	LUKE	JOHN
15. Feast for the Poor			14:12-14	
16. Tower and King			14:28-33	
17. Fig Tree	24:32-35	13:28-31	21:29-33	
18. The Porter	24:42	13:33-37	21:36	
19. The Wise Master	24:43-44			
20. The Wise Servant	24:45-51			
21. Sheep and Goats	25:31-33			

Some of the Discourses of Jesus

Sermon on the Mount. Matthew 5, 6, 7.
Address on the Mission of the Twelve. Matthew 10.
Discourse on Healing. John 5.
Discourse on the Bread of Life. John 6.
Discourse on Forgiveness. Matthew 18.
The Vine and the Branches. John 15.
The Message of Comfort for the Disciples. John 16.

VI. JESUS' TEACHING ABOUT THE KINGDOM OF GOD

"And Jesus went about all the cities and villages, teaching in their synagogues, and preaching the gospel of the kingdom."—Matthew 9:35.

Matthew 5:1—8:1; 9:35—11:1; 14:1-12
Mark 6:6-29
Luke 9:1-9

As Jesus went about doing good with the use of his healing power, his ministrations took him to many places and confronted him with many types of human need. The heavy demands for cures and the resulting tendency on the part of the multitudes to seek of him nothing but cures called forth some changes in his itinerary. More and more the method of Jesus' teaching turned to figures of speech and parables in the face of growing opposition. Amid these changes, there was a central and abiding core. Jesus lived and taught the reality of the Kingdom of God.

As a part of the training of the twelve disciples Jesus sent them out on a missionary tour. This was no doubt a step in their training, but it was also a means of preparing the way for Jesus to give himself more fully to the teaching of the Kingdom of God. In sending them out Jesus instructed them to say: "The kingdom of heaven is at hand." Jesus thus invited the disciples to begin taking a real share in the Kingdom cause.

The emphasis of Jesus' teaching with reference to the Kingdom of God varied from time to time. Beginning with the mission of the twelve disciples, his primary emphasis was on the individual in the Kingdom. Probably by this time Jesus had seen that there would be no quick turning of the multitudes to his teaching.

The idea of the Kingdom of God was not new in itself. John came preaching that such a kingdom was at hand. It reached back behind John to the long past and it represented the new era to which the Jews had looked forward since the early days of Abraham. Jesus took the idea, lived it out, and sought to acquaint both the multitudes and his disciples with its nature and its value.

From the first, some people began to notice that there was a marked difference between Jesus and John in their teaching. The specific point of difference was, "Why do your disciples not fast?" This question was asked by John's disciples (Matt. 9:14) and the Pharisees (Luke 5:33). In answer Jesus gave himself to the subject of "What is new about the Kingdom of God, and the relation of the new and the old." He had already experienced the conflict between the old and the new; and from the first he had not hesitated to admit that there was a conflict.

In seeking to unfold the meaning of the Kingdom of God, Jesus had to meet minds that already entertained a vision of a kingdom. It was wholly unlike the one he proclaimed. They were looking for a sword and he had only a loving, healing hand. He thus addressed himself to the task of emphasizing the Kingdom's orderly, expansive, and sure development; its nature and its worth.

The Sermon on the Mount deals with the kind of righteousness inherent in the Kingdom of God: its character, its relation to the old Law of Moses, its judgment, and the duty of righteousness imposed on those knowing of the reign of God. One very obvious question

was, "How much is demanded of men for their entrance?" Here
we find a dual theme: the goodness of God and the imperative of
man's faith in God's mercy.

In the last days of Jesus' ministry, when the tide has definitely
turned against him, his teaching about the Kingdom gives more emphasis to the judgment of God in which some will be shut out and
some will get into a real participating position with reference to the
Kingdom. While this element of judgment is present, the Father-
hood of God guarantees the sure coming of the Kingdom.

These questions then press us for an answer as we look at Jesus'
teaching about the Kingdom as a whole:

What is the Kingdom of God like?

    Matthew 5, 6, 7.

    Mark 4:26-32; Matthew 13:31-33, 44-50.

    See article, "Kingdom," in Westminster Bible dictionary (pp.
    344-345).

    Dummelow: "The Sermon on the Mount" (pp. 636-638).

How does the Kingdom of God differ from a kingdom built
around the Mosaic Law?

    Matthew 5:17-48.

    See Dummelow, comments on Matthew 5:17-48 (pp. 641-644).

Who are to share in the Kingdom?

    Matthew 5:3-12.

    See Dummelow, comments on the Beatitudes (pp. 638-640).

What does the Kingdom demand of its citizens?

    Matthew 6:1—7:27; 25:31-46.

How much comes from God?

    Luke 11:5-13.

What is man's part in God's Kingdom?

    Luke 15:1-10; Matthew 25:14-30; 13:3-9; 13:18-23.

What will happen to those who neglect and reject it?

    Matthew 25:1-13; Luke 14:15-24.

VII. JESUS' ENEMIES

"And there was much murmuring among the multitudes concerning him."—John 7:12.
"And some of them would have taken him."—John 7:44.

Matthew 14:13—16:12
Mark 6:30—8:26
John 6:1—7:1

At the end of the second year of Jesus' ministry the tide turned against him. The five thousand who were filled with bread thought they had found the political messiah they wanted. Jesus had left no room for such misunderstanding, but the spirit of the multitude demanded definite action. Therefore when the fragments of the feast had been gathered up he told them plainly what to expect of him. When the multitudes learned that Jesus' mission was utterly different from their expectations they began to go away.

Some, of course, suspected Jesus from the beginning. When his following began to grow there was increasing fear on the part of the political interests that Jesus would lead a revolution. This would cause Rome to act, or else those in league with Rome would lose their high positions. This opposition seems to have been stimulated, however, by the religious leadership of the day.

The religious leaders had followed Jesus carefully. They saw in him one who violated every idea they held of the Messiah. They thought him a gross sinner. They did not like his humble origin. His associates marked him as a man who had little respect for the high walls between the Jews and those who were not Jews. He even ate with publicans and sinners and went into their homes for visits. His choice of the twelve disciples did not please the religious leaders. He apparently disregarded all the sacred religious rituals and was guilty of breaking their traditions of the Sabbath. In addition he taught men to follow his example. His miracles even implied a league with the devil.

All these things began to add up, so that the Pharisees and the scribes began an open investigation of Jesus' disciples. Very shortly they began to investigate Jesus himself. So Jesus began to teach the disciples "that the Son of man must suffer many things, and be rejected by the elders, and the chief priests, and the scribes, and be killed." (Mark 8:31.)

The opposition of Jesus was on three fronts. It came from the multitudes generally as they were fired by the religious leaders; it came from the political leaders as they were excited by the religious leaders; and it came from the religious leaders in their own name. The real opposition Jesus encountered came from the supposedly good religious leadership of his day.

Some of the important questions that emerge are:

Why should a character like Jesus encounter opposition?

Would such a character excite hostility today?

What selfish motives led the people to follow and finally to reject Jesus?

> Mark 1:33-34; 2:1-2; John 6:22-71; Mark 12:7; John 12:17-18.
> Dummelow: "The Bread of Life" (pp. 784-787).

What demands in Jesus' teachings were most offensive?

> Matthew 15:1-20; 23:1-36.
> Dummelow: "The Traditions of the Elders" (pp. 677-678); "Denunciation of the Pharisees" (pp. 699-701).

To what extent were the rank and file opposed to Jesus?

Why did Jesus' home-town folk reject him?

> Luke 4:16-30; Mark 6:1-6; Matthew 13:54-58.
> See article, "Nazareth," in Westminster Bible dictionary (p. 419).

Who were the real enemies of Jesus, and what were their positions in society?

> Mark 8:11-38; John 10:22-39; John 8:21-59; John 11:45-53; John 11:54-57; Matthew 26:1-5; Matthew 27:62-66.
> See articles, "Pharisees" (p. 476), "Sadducees" (p. 524), "Herodians" (p. 241), in Westminster Bible dictionary.

Who was the first to suggest that Jesus be put to death?

> John 11:47-53.

What happened to the disciples as opposition to Jesus increased?

> Matthew 16:21-28; 17:22-23; 26:31-35, 69-75.

VIII. JESUS' DISCIPLES

"And he ordained twelve, that they should be with him, and that he might send them forth to preach."—Mark 3:14.

Matthew 16:13—18:35
Mark 8:27—9:50
Luke 9:18-62

The response of people generally to Jesus' healing and teaching was discouraging. They misinterpreted his deeds and refused his teachings. They followed from wholly selfish motives. This began to show up vividly during the last six to nine months of Jesus' work in Galilee. As a result Jesus turned most of his effort toward training the disciples. A new emphasis was beginning to appear, namely, a preparation of the disciples for the fact that Jesus would be crucified.

That Jesus intended to train an inner circle of disciples appears very early in his work. His rejection by the multitudes and the imminence of the crucifixion caused Jesus to enter upon this more intensive period in their training.

Some of those who were to share in this special training began their association with Jesus immediately after his baptism by John. As Jesus journeyed around, specific invitations were given to a number of other followers to join the inner circle. Twelve of the inner circle were appointed apostles. Much of their early training was in the listening to Jesus' teachings and the witnessing of his miracles.

One part of their training consisted of a missionary tour. They came back with startling reports of the mighty works they had been enabled to achieve. But they were not ready for the crucifixion experience. They refused to talk about it. They saw a very different outcome for Jesus. They refused to anticipate any test such as actually came when Jesus was crucified.

Four things stand out in Jesus' relationship to the disciples through the three years of association and training. First, Jesus made a careful selection of the disciples. The group he picked had real possibilities. Secondly, he taught them directly in the matter of personal character traits, in attitudes toward others, in appreciation of religious ritual and customs, and in the basic content of what was to become the Christian faith. In the third place, he made large use of daily association and companionship as a method of influence. He gave them an example. In the fourth place, he definitely laid upon them a sense of mission and in the end specifically commissioned them to go into all the world to make disciples of all men.

There were two stages in their training. The first stage pictures them essentially as learners. In the second stage they were ordained to teach what they had learned and would learn with the coming of the Comforter.

Numerous questions grow out of this brief review of Jesus and his disciples in the Gospels:

Why did Jesus set about a program for the training of a small circle of disciples?

    John 1:9-51; Matthew 4:18-22.

    See articles, "Disciple" (p. 140) and "Apostle" (pp. 35-36), in Westminster Bible dictionary.

What kind of persons did Jesus select for disciples?

    Matthew 10:2-6; Mark 3:7-19.

    Look up disciples by name in Westminster Bible dictionary.

What did the disciples expect to accomplish in following Jesus?

    Mark 9:33-37; 10:35-45.

What were the chief ideas in Jesus' definite teaching of the disciples?

What ideas did the disciples entertain which Jesus sought to correct?

    Mark 8:14—9:50; Luke 9:18-50; Matthew 16:5—18:35.

What methods did Jesus use in the training of the twelve?

    Matthew 10:5-15; 13:10-23; 14:13-21; 16:13-20; 17:1-8; John 13:1-20; 14:1-31.

What is the meaning of the final commission of the twelve disciples?

    Matthew 28:16-20; Mark 16:14-20; Luke 24:44-53.

IX. JESUS' REVELATION OF THE FATHER

"I came out from the Father . . . and go unto the Father."—John
16:28.

Matthew 19:1—20:34
Mark 10:1-52
Luke 9:51—19:28
John 7:10—11:54

Jesus left Galilee for good. Straightway he set his face toward Jerusalem, and was rejected by the Samaritans while en route. He arrived in Jerusalem during the Feast of the Tabernacles. Here Jesus
offered himself as the light of the world. He was accused of bearing
witness of himself. Jesus responded by saying: "I am he that beareth
witness of myself, and the Father that sent me beareth witness of
me." (John 8:18.) With this event Jesus began to accent more definitely the fact that he had come to reveal the Father. In this period
we have some of the great parables on the nature of God as Father;
the prayer example given to the disciples; and several insights into
the prayer life of Jesus.

The multitudes did not see clearly all that Jesus saw in his power
to do mighty works and speak truth that would make men free. Behind and within these we have the central idea that he was carrying
on the Father's work. The idea was introduced first of all at an early
age when he said, "Knew ye not that I must be about my Father's
business." (Luke 2:49, margin.) The idea was also in his last utter-
ance, "Father, into thy hands I commend my spirit." (Luke 23:46.)

The importance of this idea of God as the Father is seen in particular in Jesus' prayer habits. Prayer for Jesus was not an end in
itself, it was a way of fellowship with the Father. Through this fellowship he sought the will and power of God for specific deeds and
for his general life movement. Before all major decisions we find
Jesus retiring for prayer fellowship with his Father. The disciples saw
this frequently enough to begin to put things together. The example
Jesus gave them was implemented by direct teaching on the subject.

The relation of Jesus and the Father is seen even more clearly in the recorded prayers of Jesus. Most of them are very short, but they all emphasize that Jesus prayed to a Father-God.

In seeking to give the disciples assurance at the time of his departure, the central security Jesus pointed to was that he came from the Father and that he would return to the Father. For Jesus the crucifixion was a way to the Father.

Three central truths are involved in a study of Jesus and the Father. (1) Jesus' own relationship to the Father. (2) His teaching aimed at encouraging people in general to believe that he was the Son of God. (3) His teaching that his Father is our Father.

Some of the important questions are:

In what ways did Jesus recognize this to be his Father's world in every respect?

John 10:22-39; 17:1-26.

Dummelow: "Christ's High-priestly Prayer" (pp. 803-804).

To what extent did Jesus live his life under the realization that he was always about his Father's work?

Luke 2:49; Luke 23:46.

What help did Jesus seek from the Father?

Luke 3:21-22; Mark 1:35; 3:13-19; Matthew 14:22-23; Luke 10:21-24.

What kind of relationship to his Father did he teach the disciples to anticipate and cultivate?

Luke 11:5-13; John 11:17-46.

What personal habits toward knowing the Father's will did Jesus hold up to the disciples?

Matthew 6:5-15; 11:25-30; 26:36-46; 27:46; Luke 23:34, 46; John 11:41-42; 12:27-28; 17:1-26.

What help were the disciples to expect of the Father?

John 14:1-31.

What conditions were the disciples taught to fulfill as they sought to pray to the Father?

John 4:21-24; 9:31.

X. JESUS' FRIENDS

"Now Jesus loved Martha, and her sister, and Lazarus."—John 11:5.

Matthew 21:1—26:46
Mark 11:1—14:42
Luke 19:29—22:46
John 11:55—18:1

When Jesus was on his way to Jerusalem for the last time he arrived at Bethany six days before the Passover. Here Jesus made his
residence during the Passion week, instead of in Jerusalem. In the
daytime he went into Jerusalem, but at night he returned with his
disciples to Bethany. This was the home town of some of his friends
—Mary, Martha, and Lazarus. Three visits to these friends are recorded within the six months preceding the crucifixion. On one of
the visits Jesus had raised Lazarus from the dead. These nights in
Bethany were a striking contrast to the days spent in Jerusalem.
Here Jesus was among friends. There he was among those who were
plotting to get rid of him.

Jesus had a number of friends like Mary, Martha, and Lazarus.
During the week of his severe trials and the certainty of the cross a
number of these friends lent a helping hand. Others did not show
up as friends until after his crucifixion. These friends were strangely
silent. We know little of the conversations that took place. The
records tell us, however, some of the deeds of these friends.

A friend furnished a colt for his triumphal entry; a friend furnished a large upper room for the Passover supper with the disciples;
a friend ventured into the garden at the time of his arrest. After the
crucifixion a number of women friends made preparations to take
care of the body; a friend furnished a tomb; and another friend furnished a large amount of embalming spice.

Some of the questions that come to mind are:

Who were some of the friends of Jesus, and what did they see in
him?

John 12:1-11; John 3:1-21; 7:50-52; 19:39; Luke 10:38-42; Matthew 26:6-13.

In what ways did Jesus' friends seek to show their desire to help?
Luke 17:29-36; Mark 14:12-16; Mark 14:51-52.
What were the friends of Jesus concerned about after his crucifixion?

Matthew 27:55-61; Luke 23:50-56; Mark 15:40-47; John 19:25, 38-42.

Why did some of these friends not get a place among the disciples?
Why didn't these friends try to save Jesus from the crucifixion?

General References

See "Mary of Bethany" (p. 381) and "Nicodemus" (p. 427) in Westminster Bible dictionary.

XI. JESUS' CRUCIFIXION

"And they crucified him."—Mark 15:25

Matthew 26:47—27:66
Mark 14:43—15:47
Luke 22:47—23:56
John 18:2—19:42

The trial of Jesus may be regarded as a part of the crucifixion. It was only a pretense at an effort to deal justly with Jesus. Behind and within the trial there was considerable foul play and careful strategy on the part of those who had determined to kill Jesus.

On Tuesday evening of the Passion week the decision had been made. Judas became involved and sold himself as the one to betray Jesus. Jesus knew that his hour had come, so two days later preparations were made for the celebration of the Passover supper with the disciples. From the supper they went to the garden, where Jesus offered his intercessory prayer. This was Thursday night, and at this time and in this place Jesus was arrested. The disciples made some effort to resist the officers, but Jesus gave himself into their hands.

While considerable detail is given concerning the trial of Jesus, the actual time of the trial and the crucifixion was less than twenty-four hours. This suggests something of a mob spirit on the part of those who were hastening him to his death.

The steps in the trial seem to be as follows:

1. Jesus' examination by Annas. John 18:13-14, 19-24.
2. Jesus' examination by the Sanhedrin and the mocking. Matthew 26:57, 59-68; Mark 14:53, 55-65; Luke 22:54, 63-65.
3. Jesus condemned by the Sanhedrin. Matthew 27:1; Mark 15:1; Luke 22:66-71.
4. First appearance before Pilate, who seeks his release. Matthew 27:2, 11-14; Mark 15:1-5; Luke 23:1-7; John 18:28-38.
5. Jesus before Herod. Luke 23:6-12.
6. Second appearance before Pilate, who again tries to release him. Matthew 27:15-26; Mark 15:6-15; Luke 23:13-25; John 18:39-40.
7. Pilate's delivery of Jesus to death and scourging. Matthew 27:26-30; Mark 15:15-19; John 19:1-3.
8. Pilate makes a final effort to release Jesus. John 19:4-16.
9. Jesus led to the crucifixion. Matthew 27:31-34; Mark 15:20-23; Luke 23:26-33; John 19:16-17.

Some of the questions to be asked:

Why did Jesus submit to his arrest and crucifixion?
   Luke 9:18-27, 43-45; 18:31-34; John 14:27-31; 18:2-11.
What happened to the disciples during the arrest, trial, and crucifixion of Jesus?
   John 18:2-11, 15-18, 25-27; Matthew 26:56; 27:3-10; John 19:26-27.
Why was crucifixion used as a form of death?
   See "Crucifixion," in Westminster Bible dictionary (p. 122).
   See Dummelow, comment on Matthew 27:31-34 (p. 716).
Why did Pilate yield to the demands of the Jews?
   Matthew 27:1-2, 11-26; John 19:1-16.
What were the concerns of Jesus during the crucifixion?
   Luke 23:34-43; John 19:26-27; Matthew 27:46-47; John 19:28-30; Luke 23:46.
What part did the crowd play in enabling the enemies to carry out their plot?
   John 18:19-23; 18:39—19:16; Luke 23:13-27; Matthew 27:39-40.
What were the charges brought against Jesus?
   Luke 22:66-71; 23:1-7; John 18:7-9, 29-30.
What did Jesus' enemies hope to accomplish by crucifying him?

XII. JESUS' RESURRECTION

"Go ye therefore . . . and lo, I am with you always."—Matthew
28:19-20.

Matthew 28:1-20
Mark 16:1-20
Luke 24:1-53
John 20:1—21:25

The trial and resurrection of Jesus are related events in his life. One
represents man's desperate effort to stop the spread of his gospel and
to put him out of the way for all time. The other represents God's
certain grace, mercy, glory, and power, and his purpose to give Christ
to the world for all time.

The cruel steps leading to the crucifixion are important. More important was Jesus' willingness to finish the work of the Father. Another thing to be noted is the extent of God's love for mankind. This
is seen in God's complete giving of his Son, and in his raising his
Son from the dead.

Jesus had said that after three days he would rise from the dead.
The disciples did not understand this. Some of the Pharisees were
more fearful about it. They went so far as to persuade Pilate to seal
the tomb. This action and the unbelief of the disciples did not change
the outcome.

During the three days between the crucifixion and the resurrection
the disciples seemed to be completely discouraged. A few friends
were concerned with a decent burial. The multitudes melted away.

On the morning of the third day after the crucifixion the friends of
Jesus went to the tomb with embalming materials, to find the tomb
empty and Christ risen. For forty days Jesus appeared to various
groups. A possible order of his appearances runs as follows:

To Mary Magadalene. John 20:11-18.

To women returning from the tomb. Matthew 28:9-10.

To Peter. Luke 24:33-34; I Corinthians 15:5.

To disciples on the Emmaus road. Luke 24:13-35.

To the apostles except Thomas. Luke 24:36-43; John 20:19-24.

After eight days, Jesus appeared again to the disciples and this time Thomas was present. John 20:26-29.

Then there were a number of appearances in Galilee, whither the disciples had gone.

The appearance to seven disciples by the sea. John 21.

The appearance to about 500. I Corinthians 15:6.

The appearance to James. I Corinthians 15:7.

The appearance to the eleven, and the Great Commission. Matthew 28:16-20; Luke 24:44-49; Acts 1:8.

The last appearance to the disciples and the ascension. Luke 24:50-53; Acts 1:9-11.

There is an intimate story behind most of these appearances, such as to Peter, James, and Mary. Fellowship that had been broken was being restored and renewed. Problems that had been hidden were brought to light. Jesus who had been crucified walked and talked with his disciples again.

Some of the questions to be asked are:

Why did the disciples refuse to heed Jesus' frequent reference to his death and resurrection?

Matthew 16:21-26; Luke 9:43-45.

When Jesus was crucified, why did the disciples go back to their fishing, apparently turning completely away from Jesus?

John 21:1-4.

What did Jesus teach during the period between his resurrection and the ascension?

John 20:16-18; Luke 24:25-27; Luke 24:38-48; John 20:21-23; John 20:26-29; John 21; Mark 16:15-18.

What did the disciples gain, in the way of a sense of Jesus' continuing presence, through the appearances?

Note references listed with the appearances above.

Where do we find the disciples after Jesus gave them the Great Commission and ascended into heaven?

Luke 24:50-53; Mark 16:19-20; Acts 1:9-14.

Is he our Risen Lord?

THE ACTS

CHARACTERISTICS of the EARLY CHURCH

PATRICK D. MILLER

THE ACTS

CHARACTERISTICS OF THE EARLY CHURCH

THE ACTS

I. INTRODUCTORY STATEMENT

Dr. Floyd V. Filson in his book, *One Lord—One Faith,* says, "The Primitive Church" (he means from the resurrection to about A.D. 50) "has often failed to receive the intensive study it deserves. Books dealing with the history of the New Testament Church have usually touched lightly upon this primitive period and hastened on to the surer ground of the career of Paul." The present study of the Acts will therefore deal primarily with chapters 1—12, which cover that period before Paul emerged as the leader of the Gentile church. Some of the things which occurred in those early days need to happen in our day; we need a return to the opening chapters of Acts for the testing of our modern churches and for the warming of our own souls.

The Book of the Acts

1. NAME. In the King James Version it is "The Acts of the Apostles." In some of the best manuscripts it is "Acts of Apostles," or simply "Acts." The book does not contain all the acts of any apostle, but only the main line of events in the early church as they were known to the author and as the Spirit led him to write. For that reason the American Standard Version is more accurate in giving the name, "The Acts." The original manuscript was lost and so we do not know what the author did originally call it. From the emphasis given to the leadership of the Spirit, he might well have named the book, "The Acts of the Holy Spirit."

2. AUTHOR. The name of the author is not given, but the following points are taken to establish his identity:

a. He was with Paul a part of the time. (See the "we" sections, 16:10; 20:6, etc.)

b. He was not Barnabas or John Mark because we know they had parted from Paul before the "we" sections appear.

c. He was not Silas or Timothy because these are always referred to in the third person.

d. He could hardly have been Titus, for Titus was with Paul before the "we" sections begin. (See Gal. 2:3.)

e. He must then have been Luke, the author of the third Gospel. We reach this conclusion because of the language used and the address to Theophilus, together with the testimony of the early church fathers.

f. What we know about Luke.

(1) He was not an eyewitness of Jesus (Luke 1:2.)

(2) He was not a Jew. (See Colossians 4:10-14 and note that Luke is not listed with those "of the circumcision.")

(3) He introduces himself first at Troas (16:8-10); he journeyed with Paul to Rome (27:1); and was doubtless with him to the end (II Timothy 4:11, "Only Luke is with me").

(4) Tradition says he himself suffered martyrdom in Gaul.

(5) We conclude that he was thoroughly acquainted with the early church both from observation and inquiry; that he deeply loved our Lord; and that he was wondrously modest in telling of his own part in this drama of events.

3. Place and Date. Acts was most probably written at Rome about A.D. 63 or 64, near the time of Paul's death. It must have been written for Gentile believers and is addressed to Theophilus, who was probably a Roman official whom Luke will not identify further because of the danger it might involve. The time covered by the book is about 30 years, A.D. 33-63.

4. Purpose of the Book. The points of emphasis given here may be illustrated by many references.

a. One purpose must have been to show that *the same Jesus who died and rose again was continuing to lead his church*. Note how often the apostles acted against their natural judgment and inherited prejudices because they believed the living Lord was leading them to do certain things.

b. Another purpose was to show that *the living Lord was present in his church through the Holy Spirit*.

c. Another purpose was to show *how the New Testament church began.* Note that Luke's Gospel tells what "Jesus began" and the Acts what his followers began under the leadership of the Holy Spirit. Behold how much has grown from those right beginnings! Surely all that Jesus aims to be and do in us is but begun here in this life.

d. Another purpose, as we can see now, was to *bridge the gap between the Gospels and the Epistles.* Much of what Peter, Paul, James, and John wrote to various groups in the form of letters would be unintelligible to us except for the record of Acts.

e. The grand purpose is *to show the conquest of the gospel from Jerusalem to Rome.*

5. STRUCTURE OF THE BOOK. The simple structure of the book sets forth the grand purpose of the author. Note how the outline flows from 1:8.

a. The Church in Jerusalem. Chapters 1—7.
b. The Church Spreading Into Judea and Samaria. Chapters 8-12.
c. The Church Spreading Across the Gentile World. Chapters 13—28.

The Procedure

The book of Acts could be studied chapter by chapter. It could be approached from the standpoint of its missionary message. A fine study could be worked out on the Holy Spirit in Acts, and another on the sermons and orations in the book. We will, however, limit ourselves here to some characteristics of the early church as seen in Acts. Read the first twelve chapters straight through and then ask yourself what you have discovered about that early church.

II. A CHURCH OF ORDINARY PEOPLE

We who make up the church of today are prone to conclude that the achievements of the church in Acts are quite impossible in the present because we feel that we have now no such good people. One is neither critical nor irreverent when he, as a plain garden-variety Christian of today, points out how like ourselves these early believers were. See what patience our Lord had to exercise before he brought them to his ideals. Note, for example, the kind of people with which the church began.

People Who Thought They Already Knew

1. ALL ABOUT THE KINGDOM EXCEPT WHEN IT WAS TO BE ESTAB-
LISHED. (1:6.) They shared the then current Jewish belief that the
Messiah would erect an earthly kingdom at Jerusalem and conquer
all their foes. They had gotten their ideas from Jewish apocalyptic
literature—most of which was never accounted worthy of a place in
the canon of the Old Testament—and must have paid scant attention to what Jesus told them "concerning the kingdom of God."
(1:3.) They were asking (Greek tense indicates asking over and
over) for a timetable on *when* Jesus was going to do this thing they
were so sure he would do. Small wonder he rebuked them for their
cocksureness as well as for their curiosity concerning a nonessential
to his plan. Jesus did not say "times" and "seasons" are unimpor-
tant; he said they are matters God has marked "personal," and therefore are things man is not to tamper with. For the furthering of
Christ's real purpose and spiritual kingdom it was not a timetable
they needed but power to witness. They were to be spiritually ener-
gized witnesses to a personal Saviour from sin, and not stargazing
date-fixers stirring up profitless curiosity about things which the
Father had in his own keeping.

2. HOW TO FILL THE VACANCY IN THE APOSTOLATE. The little
band proceeded to choose a successor to Judas *before* the Spirit had
descended and with no warrant beyond Peter's quotation from
Psalms 69 and 109. (Ps. 69:25; 109:8.) It need not be said that they
made a mistake in selecting Matthias, but we certainly hear no
more of him after this day and we find no occasion after Pentecost
when the Christian church cast lots to discover the will of God.
Maybe the robes of office just smothered Matthias; maybe the real successor God was preparing was a Pharisee named Saul. We like Justus,
the defeated candidate; he did not insist even upon being made a
deacon. The church has run ahead of the Holy Spirit at times when
she would have done well to wait and be taught. Such a thing can
occur, even in calling a pastor.

People Who Could Not Always Agree

They were very human. Sometimes they were controversial, even after the Spirit had come. Note some of the times when they did not see eye to eye: Paul and Barnabas (15:36-40); Peter and the Jerusalem believers (11:1-3); Peter and Paul (Gal. 2:11).

People Who Even Proved to Be Hypocrites

We hear so much about hypocrites in the modern churches that one would suppose it was peculiar to our day. Note Ananias and Sapphira (5:1-11), and Simon the sorcerer (8:9-13, 18-23). A hypocrite is one who wears a mask which hides his real likeness. The one who points out the presence of hyprocrites in the church as his reason for not being a Christian may be wearing a mask himself and hiding behind this as an excuse to go on following his own low desires. There were, and still are, hypocrites *within* and *without* the visible church. Let that deter no man from following Christ.

People of the Narrowest Outlook

The first Christians were mostly Jews and they had a lot of inherited narrowness to overcome before Christ's mind could become theirs. To them all other people on earth were Gentile dogs. What soul growth they had to experience before they could think of every man as the "brother for whom Christ died"!

The early church did begin with people who were far from perfect. But our Lord had great faith in ordinary, fallible folks such as these. For just such people he had died; with them he started the most revolutionary movement ever known; and upon them as first members he built a church against which the very gates of hell can never prevail. What comfort and encouragement for us who know our own frailties! Imperfect people always make up Christ's church here, but when he has finished in us his good work of grace, the very same people will make up the church which he will deliver to the Father "not having spot or wrinkle."

III. A PRAYING CHURCH

The modern church is prepared to go forward spirtually in about the same proportion to the earnestness with which she looks backward to the New Testament church for the divine pattern of procedure. It it just as sensible for us to depend upon these things as it is for a modern machine farmer to depend still on such old-fashioned things as rain and sunshine. You may dress a sailor up in an Admiral's uniform and put him on the greatest vessel afloat and he will still need to know the tides, the stars, and the compass. These are old-fashioned things, but they are still essential to life at sea. When we return to the early church for a pattern of procedure it is evident at once that this was a *praying group*. We do not attempt here to discuss prayer theoretically or to dwell on our need for prayer. Let us look at this group actually praying and see what is suggested for us and our congregations.

See How Often They were in Prayer

Go right through Acts and make a list of the times and circumstances which called the church members to prayer. Since these 28 chapters cover some thirty years, we may safely assume that this is a very incomplete list. It is, however, a very suggestive one.

See More Closely the First Prayer Gathering

Note how much we can learn about their praying in the upper room. (1:14.) These early believers were learning the secret of prayer.

1. THEY WERE TOGETHER. "These all with one accord." They were not simply all physically present in one place—though even that is more than we usually achieve at prayer meetings. These words indicate that they were together in the deeper sense of *mind* and *sympathy* and *mutual interest*. Nor was that any superficial thing, easy to accomplish. Look what *diverse minds* had come together in the high exercise of prayer.

a. The apostles, who but a few months before had been jealously eyeing one another and coveting the best places in the expected kingdom. Study these eleven men and see how unlike they were and then see how the differences disappear in the act of united prayer.

b. The women, some of whom had very unenviable records. Here the forgiven woman of the street and the lovely sisters of Bethany were united in prayer.

c. Mary, the mother of Jesus, who had once thought him mad, is now praying in his name—not being adored herself, but adoring him as any other believer.

d. His brethren who had not believed while he was alive are now united in prayer with all the others. Behold how much had been forgiven and forgotten and washed away in this new experience. It must have been so before these "all with one accord" could pray. The condition still stands: "If two of you shall agree." "If ye forgive not." "Forgive us our debts, *as* we forgive." What a lesson for divided congregations, divided social groups, and divided Christendom!

2. THEY WERE BESIEGING GOD. These who were thus united "continued stedfastly" in prayer. These very words are used elsewhere in the Greek to describe the action of an army besieging a walled city. Now how is a city taken by force of arms? Surely not by surrounding it and timidly asking for entrance. This little band had their marching orders from Christ and they knew how impossible was their task unless God should empower them to face that pagan world. Under the sense of joy over the Risen Lord, and need for new power, they "continued stedfastly" in prayer. Such moral earnestness belongs to all prayer that would reach to God. How disturbing it is to ask if this marks our praying today!

3. THEY WERE HEARD OF GOD. We get little information here on just what they asked for. They were praying, and real prayer is always so much more than merely "asking for things." We have put it on that plane so often that our children may easily come to think of God as a sort of glorified groceryman with whom one stops doing business when the goods are not delivered promptly and as specified in the order. One can imagine some of the praise and thanksgiving and petition in that upper room. But no matter now what they prayed for; the point is that *God heard their sort of praying.* Witness the fact that within a few days a mighty new power was loosed

among them; the 120 became 3,120 in a day; and that cleansing fire began which has now burned clear across the world and down nineteen centuries to us.

Whatever else they were or did, this early group made up a praying church. Perhaps therein lay the real secret of their mighty accomplishments for God in the spread of the gospel of his Son, our Saviour.

IV. A DEMOCRATIC CHURCH

Martin Luther broke with the Roman Church on doctrine and returned to the Scriptures as the authority on all such questions. Calvin and the later Reformers sought to re-establish a more scriptural form of church government. When one reads the record he is struck with how *simple* and *democratic* was the procedure of this early church. If a hierarchy ever should run the church, surely this would have been the time, while the apostles were alive and in their prime. Were there "princes of the church" then, or was it the simple democratic fellowship most Protestants believe the church should be? In an attempt to answer that question let us look at the way they did some things here in Acts.

The Group in the Upper Room. 1:12-14.

1. Read the passage and note again who were present that day.

2. Examine the record carefully and see if it does not indicate that they were all together on a *plane of equality.*

The Election of Matthias. 1:15-26.

1. Note that while Peter presides and makes a short speech, he does not attempt to decide for the group who should fill the vacancy left by Judas' defection.

2. Neither did the apostles as a body attempt to fill the vacancy. The decision was left to the ordinary believers—the 123 members present at the congregational meeting, including *even the women.*

The Experience of Pentecost. 2:1-4.

1. We read that they were "all together"; that the power of God

came alike upon "each one of them"; and that "they were all filled with the Holy Spirit."

2. We read that Peter stood up to speak "with the eleven" and not alone as the prince among the apostles. In this connection it should be borne in mind that Peter was perhaps the eldest; that they always had due respect for age; and that he was *always ready* to speak before anyone else, even at times when he did not know what he was talking about and had to be severely rebuked. (Matt. 16:21 ff.)

The Election of Deacons. 6:1-8.

1. Note that they were chosen "from among" the brethren to attend to the material side of the Christian enterprise in Jerusalem.

2. The apostles committed this momentous choice directly to the congregation. "Look ye out . . . from among you . . . and . . . the whole multitude . . . chose . . ."

3. The apostles then had prayer and laid hands upon these men in the simple sort of ordination service such as can be seen now in the churches of many denominations.

Events Following the Conversion of Paul. Chapter 9.

1. The greatest preacher in all history was baptized and had the laying on of hands by an otherwise unknown disciple named Ananias.

2. No apostle was called to Damascus for this consecration. The original apostles were not even consulted!

Barnabas at Antioch. 11:19-26; 13:1-3.

1. Note that it was the "church which was in Jerusalem," and not the apostles, who sent Barnabas on this very important mission.

2. See him go to Tarsus and ask Paul to come to Antioch without so much as a word from the Jerusalem powers.

3. Then see the church at Antioch on its own authority ordain and send out Paul and Barnabas as missionaries.

Reviewing the procedure in this period we may safely conclude that there were no princes of the church in that day, and there need be none now. No apology is ever necessary for the simple, democratic forms of government found in the Protestant churches.

V. AN EMPOWERED CHURCH

This early church became a channel for God's power in the world. Of course it did. Something like this will always happen when men are before God in moral earnestness and in a sense of their own deep need. The way is open then for God to come, and when *he* comes there is *power*. This infant church of the open heart did receive God's power in grand measure. Evidence of the life changes thus wrought is upon every page of the New Testament.

The Nature of This Power in the Church

Men of our day pay homage to all power that gets things done. We look at a great piece of machinery and marvel at the *power* in it. We look at a man who has acquired wealth with its inevitable control over the lives of men, and we say he is a man of *power*. We observe a nation massing vast arms, and we say that is *power*. With force of this kind men can and do change things, though not by any means always for the better.

That sort of outward physical power was present in the Roman Empire and the men who controlled it. Yet they were not able to destroy this little Jesus movement made up so often of the weak, the persecuted, and the poor. Some force came into that group which enabled it to withstand the Empire's persecutions and to continue to build after that Empire was gone.

What these Christians needed and what they had was *spiritual power,* which cannot be seen or counted in horsepower and dollars. For that reason, men who pride themselves upon being practical often suspect it of being unreal. But these Christians were not dealing with physical phenomena; they were trying under God to build a new sort of human society through a new sort of men and women. Jesus had promised them *power for that purpose,* and the promise was made good. The thing they received at Pentecost was unseen, but it was not unreal. A thing cannot lack reality which made cowards into brave men; which made liars and thieves into honest men; which made fearful and sad souls into brave and glad ones. What came at Pentecost was divine power let loose by God into the lives of men and women who were morally in earnest. Its purpose was not to conquer Rome—that is *physical* power, always found on earth. Its purpose was to conquer evil in the human heart and open morally blind eyes to see God—that is *spiritual* power, which must come from God.

The Source of This Power in the Church

The source has already been suggested. We read Acts 2:4, "they were all filled with the Holy Spirit."

1. The verb used here is passive and must mean that this Power came to them from an outside source, sent from God and not worked up by men.

2. The empowering was a Person—the Holy Spirit of God—whose coming is *the great event* of Acts. Pentecost is the birthday of the church's power to preach Christ.

3. What occurred at Pentecost cannot be entirely understood by us. It was not fully understood by those who experienced it. But let us never be afraid to accept the fact of Pentecost because it looks like a miracle. Pentecost itself presents no such stupendous miracle as the *change* it wrought in these Christians and the world-wide church they went forth to build. The miracle of Pentecost can still be felt in experience and seen in the Christian church.

What Every Christian Ought to Know About the Holy Spirit's Power

What we learn about the Holy Spirit in the New Testament needs to be taught to every believer. His power cannot come to a generation unaware of his presence in the world. Note at least the following:

1. The Holy Spirit came in new power as the *fulfillment* of *promises* made by Jesus as he approached the end of his earthly work. (John 14 and 16; Acts 1:8.)

2. The coming of the Holy Spirit was "expedient," that is, such an arrangement would be *an advantage* to the church. (John 16:7.) The Christ, once limited by the very flesh he had assumed, was to be reinvested with all his eternal power, glory, and grace and the Holy Spirit would mediate such a Christ to the hearts of men. The Christ

of the flesh limited to a small area of the earth would, through the Holy Spirit, be mediated to all the world and through all the generations.

3. The Holy Spirit came for *specific* and *gracious purposes* indicated by Jesus.

a. To help believers.

(1) As Consoler.

(2) As Helper.

(3) As Guide—especially in distinguishing the true from the false.

(4) As Interpreter of Christ to us.

(5) As our Aid in witnessing for Christ.

b. To convict sinners or unbelievers.

4. The Holy Spirit is *present now* and *available to every believer*. This is the age of his work and all good in Christians is the result of this presence. Wherever there is saintliness of life, witness to Jesus, and courage to carry on in dark days, there is evidence of the presence of the Holy Spirit. Surely we are not without ample evidence of his presence in our day.

5. The Holy Spirit is *indispensable now*. The most profound and baffling and perplexing problems that face man are always *moral* in nature, which means that they must be dealt with by moral and spiritual force. And God only can do that, working through his Holy Spirit in us.

6. Our need is *to be filled* with the Holy Spirit's power. How shall that be?

a. Remember that our body is the temple of the Holy Spirit and he can dwell best in a clean and holy place. How that thought searches us through!

b. Remember he came first to a sense of need. The humble and praying heart makes room for him now as it did at the first.

c. Remember he comes for right uses. When we earnestly desire his power for unselfish purposes and reach out hands to help others —then and there we most often find him present in the heart.

d. Remember that he comes most surely when we are among people of Christlike mind. These should be our preferred companions, yet there are selfish and worldly-minded folks who need our friendship and who will not know Christ unless they see him in us. We need the Holy Spirit's leading here.

e. Remember, finally, that he comes through obedience to the known will of Christ. When we are unwilling to walk with Jesus so far as we know the way, then we exclude this quiet and gracious power from our lives.

This section began by noting that the evidence of life-changing power in the early church is upon every page of the New Testament. Wherever and whenever the Holy Spirit has been present these 1900 years, there the Acts of the Apostles have been continued. Here is the only answer to the need of our day and of every day until he shall come.

VI. A HAPPY CHURCH

This primitive group lacked many of the outer trappings we are accustomed to associate with any well-organized modern church. But they were a glad and happy fellowship of those who knew themselves redeemed by the Lord Jesus and, therefore, sought to follow him. What avails it for daily living if we have buildings and liturgy and impressive numbers and still lack the central thing of a glad Christian spirit? Read this book of Acts and you will find that the note of gladness and rejoicing runs through it like a strong tide. It can be felt all the way from those first days in Jerusalem when the little band "took their food with gladness and singleness of heart" until an old man sits in his prison at Rome to write to his Philippian friends, "Christ is proclaimed; and therein I rejoice, yea, and will rejoice. . . . Finally, my brethren, rejoice in the Lord." (Phil. 1:18; 3:1.)

What produced this daily music of the soul? What changed a desolate and discouraged group so radically that in a few days it became the very center of enthusiasm and abounding good cheer? It is not hard to find the answer to such a question here in the open-ing chapters of Acts. The following was surely some of the reasons for that happiness of the early church.

They Had Seen the Risen Lord

The despair and gloom of the crucifixion day had changed into the joy of Easter morning when they knew him to be alive. When they first *heard* he was alive, they wondered and some doubted; but when he had stood in their midst and spoken in the old familiar accents, the record says, "The disciples therefore were glad, when they saw the Lord." (John 20:20.) When Peter stood up to preach his first Christian sermon, he said, "This Jesus did God raise up, whereof we all are witnesses." (Acts 2:32.)

Now all other religions of earth have failed at this point of producing happiness, because each of them ends in futility and death. Confucius is dead and his followers know it. Gautama Buddha is dead and his followers know it. But the Lord Jesus is alive forevermore *and his followers know it.* Have no doubt on this point, my friends, a joyous and victorious religion never was founded on a dead god. And if our souls sing not here and in our daily duties, if our experience is too somber and gray with no heavenly sunshine in the heart, then we might well re-examine the very foundation of our faith. This early group who ate their daily bread with gladness—who sang in a Philippian jail—who still sang their hymns of victory when hunted in the catacombs and thrown to the lions—*this group knew that Jesus lived and was present with them* in the Spirit.

They Had Settled a Perplexing Question

When the gospel had been proclaimed, the first cry of these men was, "Brethren, what shall we do?" That had been the unhappy cry of the Hebrew heart from Abraham to Jesus. Being aware in some measure of the true God, the Hebrews were always perplexed about how sinful man was ever to stand uncondemned before his holy presence. They had a priesthood and offered sacrifices of many kinds, but always the question stood—what shall we do to stand before God? It was that central question which set earnest and troubled men to trying to keep every precept of the law, together with an almost infinite number of their own petty rules. They came to be called Pharisees—the separated ones—but all their outward exercises of goodness never came within a thousand miles of satisfying sensitives and honest souls like Saul of Tarsus.

When the gospel was preached at Pentecost, the Jews cried out their age-old question, "What shall we do?" and Peter answered at once, "Repent ye, and be baptized every one of you in the name of Jesus Christ unto the remission of your sins; and ye shall receive the gift of the Holy Spirit." (Acts 2:37-38.) Here, at long last, is the answer to their ancient question of what shall be done. The answer is that God has come in Jesus and done for them what they could never do for themselves. He has taken all that which separated them from God and borne it "in his own body upon the tree." (I Peter 2:24.) The Holy Spirit took that *greatest of all truths,* and drove it home to their hearts until 3,000 at once received the truth, cast themselves in believing faith upon Jesus, and were baptized into his name. *Then* those very people began to take their food "with gladness and singleness of heart." The old struggle was over, the question of guilt and conscience had been settled; they stood before God's holiness unafraid because they knew now that his holiness was matched by his forgiving love. It was a happy church because it was made up of persons who genuinely repented or turned away from their sins and who were now sure God held no old accounts against them.

They Had Entered a Beautiful Fellowship

Man's relationship to his fellows is always determined by his relationship to God. And so when these men saw God as their forgiving Father, they began at once to see each other as brothers. Some were rich and some poor, so they pooled their resources to see that all were provided for when the coming storm of persecution should break. This Christian communism was never made obligatory upon the church, but history records that when the outside world saw these Christians have concern for one another, people began to exclaim, "Behold how they love one another!" The church was happy when members thought less of self and more of the common good; when they allowed all old grievances to be buried with their sins; when the strong sought to lift the weak instead of grinding them down; and when giving was prized as much as getting. Would God we might be as magnificently obsessed by the Spirit of Jesus as those men were. Surely we who have been forgiven enough to call God "our Father," have been forgiven enough to call all others here our brothers and sisters. A church where that spirit of fellowship prevails will be a happy church—and all men who come that way will know it.

Two very simple truths emerge from this study.

1. Happiness in itself is not the chief end of man; it is the byproduct of a certain kind of living. The chief end of man is to glorify God in faith and life. That may appear at times to lead away from happiness, but it is the only road to the real thing. Hence the disillusionment of the millions who spend billions in a ceaseless effort to buy happiness in the market. Too often the Devil owns the market and his synthetic happiness is like a beautiful bubble that passes out of sight when we grasp it. True happiness cannot be worked up; it cannot be purchased with money; it cannot be manufactured with alcohol. It is a by-product of living by faith in God a clean, wholesome, useful life.

2. It follows that true happiness is most often to be found in the common, everyday events of life. It springs from within and for that reason can be had at home just as easily as away at some new place. These early Christians shared what they had; they went together to worship at certain regular times; they visited in one another's homes; they went about their daily work—*and in that they were happy*. Here is one of life's profoundest secrets and one we need to discover again. Jesus came with power to redeem all of life; and if we fail to find it in everyday events, we need not hope to find it in some novel and unique fashion. Our need then is neither to seek happiness as an end in itself, nor to search for any place where it abides. We need this committal of life to him who makes the heart to sing at common tasks and amid all common things.

VII. An Expanding Church

This little band of praying, Spirit-filled, happy people soon entered upon a period of marvelous growth. Of course such a church expanded. No power on earth could prevent it from doing so. The powers of earth and hell did combine to hinder it but the cause of Christ marched on.

Let us examine this growth as seen in the Acts and note a few things about it. By no means all expansion here had to do with size and numbers, though that is too largely the measure by which we now judge any church. The primitive church had a marvelous numerical growth, but some other things are equally as noticeable in Acts.

The Spiritual Growth After Pentecost

1. The spiritual growth of the church is seen in their *fuller understanding of our Lord's mission*. At Acts 1:6 we find the disciples asking a question which had little or no relevancy to the thing Christ had in mind for them to do. He had not died to build a Jewish kingdom, but to bear the penalty of man's sin and to make possible a worldwide fellowship of forgiven men. Now read Acts 2:22 ff. and see how far these men had gone in understanding the true mission of Jesus. There are no questions here, but a great affirmation of good news that the crucified and risen Christ is the power of God unto salvation for everyone that believeth.

2. This spiritual growth is seen in a *new understanding of Scripture*. Jesus had bidden them to search the Scriptures and now he had sent the Spirit to guide them into an understanding of its truth. See them here learning daily that the Old Testament testifies to Christ. Mind you, these men knew the *contents* of Scripture before, but as growing Christians they now sought its *spiritual meaning* for the needs of the hour.

3. Their spiritual growth is seen in a *new attitude toward physical danger*. At the trial and crucifixion they ran away into hiding. The upper room itself was probably first secured as a place of hiding. See them now after Pentecost preaching and testifying to the resurrection wherever men will hear them. Acts 3:1 shows them going up boldly to the Temple at the regular hour of prayer. At no time did they indulge in heroics or recklessly court danger, but *fear* was a word that seems to have lost its meaning for them.

4. Their spiritual growth is seen in *broadening human sympathies.* In a land where poverty abounded, this new fellowship saw to it at once that no humblest member should suffer need. See 2:44-45. We need not here discuss their experiment in communism of property, but we should not miss the point that the well-to-do had experienced such a growth in social sympathies that they actually sold real estate and used a part of their capital funds to meet the needs of the hour. In a land where Jews had no dealings with Samaritans or anyone else and had not had such dealings for centuries—right here we find the most radical changes taking place. These narrow, prejudiced, and nationalistic Jews were presently dealing on a basis of equality with people in Samaria, 8:14-17; in Gaza, 8:26-38; and in Caesarea, 10:1-48. Why is so much space given to this episode of Peter and the centurion unless it was intended to be a rebuke to *religious, racial, social,* or *national prejudices* whenever and wherever found? A growing Christian is one who, among other things, is learning to distinguish between his *inherited prejudices* and his *God-given principles.* Here in Acts they were doing this at a breath-taking rate.

Numerical growth is to be desired, and conservative modern churches need to give much more thought to the multitudes of unsaved all around them. The point of this particular lesson is to indicate what may be the fundamental reason for a slow growth. Wherever such expansion has slowed down we may be sure the trouble is not in the gospel; it has worked too long and has never yet lost its power to save men. We may be sure the trouble is not in unfavorable world conditions; they have never been favorable to the gospel and certainly were not in the first century. The most likely place to find the trouble is right in us who fill the church pews, teach in the church school, and preach in the pulpits. When we are not growing in grace there is little reason to expect that the church will grow in numbers.

Ponder the soul-growth of this early Spirit-filled church and you have the key to the marvelous numerical and geographical expansion which took place in the lifetime of the apostles. However humbling it may be, we do well to go back here to first principles and apply them in our own lives.

VIII. AN EXPANDING CHURCH

(Continued)

There appear to have been few, if any, statistical reports made out by the New Testament churches. That was a development of later times. There is no emphasis in the New Testament upon numbers as such. One would have to guess at the number of converts under the preaching of the Apostles. Even so, there is enough in the book of Acts to indicate that amazing numerical and geographical expansion did take place.

Numerical Growth

At the cross there was only *one*. What *courage* he had who died alone, and what *faith* in the power of his death to bring multitudes to God! At the ascension there were eleven. At the election of Matthias there were 120. After Pentecost and Peter's first sermon there were 3,120. That sounds like a magic formula, and so it was. Something comparable to geometrical progression occurred there when men who were made over by the living Christ went out to tell the good news to others. The thing was real, and real religion is contagious.

Geographical Expansion

It is doubtful if the Apostles even began to understand our Saviour when he told them in Acts 1:8 that they would be empowered to witness for him from Jerusalem out to the ends of the earth. But when his promised power came, the movement began at once to leap over all Jewish bounds. In Acts 2 we are told of more than a dozen nationalities who were touched in one day at Jerusalem. In Acts 8 we find Philip, a first deacon of the church, spreading the good news as far as Samaria and then speaking of it to an Ethiopian official away down at Gaza to the south of Jerusalem. Has a Christian traveling man any chance to touch men quietly for Christ and the better life? Go ask Philip if men did not hear him and believe. In Acts 10 we find Peter baptizing an entire Roman household down at the seaport town of Caesarea and then stoutly defending himself against those Jerusalem Jews who still felt that the gospel was for them only. When he had convinced them it was right to baptize this Gentile soldier, it is recorded that they glorified the Lord because he had granted repentance to those they had thought were outside the covenant promises.

When this tide of expansion began to move, things happened fast in that formerly narrow little Jewish group. Persecution arose in Jerusalem; and in Acts 11 we find a group of believers who had scattered away over to Syrian Antioch preaching their Jesus to cultured and sophisticated Greeks. To help them, the Jerusalem leaders sent the sweet-spirited Barnabas—he who had given his wealth to set up a trust fund for Christian work and had fully given his life to Jesus. He was able to guide the movement among cultured people like himself. Behold here a successful businessman who did not feel that living and spreading the gospel was a matter to be left to women and children only. When Barnabas had looked over the situation at Antioch, he sent across to Tarsus for a little Jew by the name of Saul —he who had come to terms with Christ on the Damascus road and is known to us as Paul. Then, in the 13th chapter of Acts, we come upon one of the crucial moments in history when Barnabas, the businessman, and Paul, the scholar, were set apart as missionaries of the movement and sent forth into the Roman world.

The day Barnabas and Paul and John Mark set sail for the island of Cyprus, that little church of the first century committed herself to an expansion program that did not cease until a Roman Caesar had exclaimed, "O Galilean, thou hast conquered!" It was a program that did not cease until the name of Jesus was known among our barbaric ancestors who then roamed the woods of northern Europe and the British Isles. It was a program that did not cease until the Pilgrim fathers had planted the cross of Christ upon these free shores of our new world. To be sure, that early church was *little,* and *insignificant,* and often *persecuted;* but she was *mighty* because she was made up of people who had found forgiveness in Christ and were wholly committed to doing his will. Moreover, at every point of history since that early day, when Christians have really been trying to follow Christ there has been a reaching out and a sending out to share this experience with others.

IX. A GENEROUS CHURCH

We have already noted something of the spiritual growth which took place in the band of early believers. Most of them were Jews and the movement began in the hitherto narrow Jewish community of Jerusalem.

One notable aspect of this soul growth that began to appear as a result of the new power received at Pentecost was the impulse to *generosity*. It is first noted in connection with the Pentecost experience and continues to appear right on through the New Testament. Acts is not a tract on the stewardship of possessions, but one who reads the book and the Epistles of Paul cannot escape the conclusion that here was a generous church. When the Holy Spirit changed these narrow Jews into Christians his gracious work did not stop short of their pocketbooks.

In the Jerusalem Fellowship

The economic life of this community was largely controlled by those who opposed and crucified Jesus. It stood to reason that men of such bitter prejudice toward him would not deal kindly with his followers. The converts on the day of Pentecost must have sensed that danger at once. So we find them banding themselves together in a fellowship of sharing, which was perhaps the purest Christian communism ever seen on earth. (2:43-47 and 4:32-37.) What they did then and there evidenced a generosity seldom seen. Most Christians are accounted generous when they give a tenth of their annual income. In this emergency the saints "sold their possessions and goods" in order that none should lack. This communism is nowhere enjoined as obligatory, and we find it soon disappeared.

In the Church at Antioch

Barnabas began his Christian testimony by selling a piece of real estate and placing the money in the church treasury in Jerusalem. After a little this same noble Barnabas was sent to direct the newly established community of believers in Syrian Antioch. (11:19 ff.) This educated businessman of large vision saw the opportunity in Antioch and went at once to Tarsus for a converted Jew by the name of Saul. Now, instead of this group calling for help, we find one of their first united undertakings was an offering for the hard-pressed brethren back in Judea. They gave, "every man according to his ability," and sent their offering by the hands of Barnabas and Saul. Whenever Christian giving is on the basis of "every man according to his ability" there will be no lack of money for the Lord's work.

In the Missionary Churches

We are not surprised to find that missionaries sent out from Antioch taught new converts the privilege and duty of generous Christian giving.

Paul pens his sublime 15th chapter of I Corinthians on the resurrection of the dead and then passes without a break to an appeal for a "collection for the saints." Moreover, he says the same instructions have been given to the churches in Galatia. (I Cor. 16:1-4.)

In II Corinthians he devotes all of chapters 8 and 9 to the matter of the offering. In II Corinthians 8:1-5 there is a touching and beautiful reference to the liberality of the churches of Macedonia. Philippians 4:10 ff. indicates that the Philippians were the leaders in this respect.

What evidence we have in the New Testament indicates that this early church was generous. Why are there not more appeals for money recorded here in the Acts? Surely not because there was little need. There was need on all sides. But few appeals were necessary because there was great generosity even in the midst of poverty. The motive to generosity has always been present and operative when the Spirit of Jesus possessed men's hearts.

X. A Bold and Daring Church

We have noted many characteristics of the early church. Surely none is more strikingly seen in the Acts than the boldness and daring of these first Christians. Cowards could never have done what they did. There was a holy boldness about them that condemns all time-serving timidity on the part of those who claim to be possessed by the explosive power of the gospel. See how this boldness was evidenced.

In Confronting the Jews with Him Whom They Had Crucified

It is no safe and easy thing to confront a mob and tell them they are wrong. As Jesus went to the cross there was no man willing to stand and defend him. Pilate, the pagan Roman, came nearer doing it than any other.

But see what happened after the resurrection, the ascension, and the descent of the Spirit. Peter, the erstwhile coward, now stands up before these very same Jerusalem Jews and declares that the man they crucified was the Messiah of prophecy. He says he knows this because God has raised Jesus from the dead. (2:22 ff.) The high church party among the Jews hated Jesus, bitterly denounced his claims, and hounded him to his death. It was something new in Jerusalem that a Galilean fisherman should stand up before these men and accuse them of murder. Nothing could so enrage them as the suggestion that this Jesus had really risen from the dead.

One is amazed at the apostles' utter disregard for public opinion and personal safety. They preach the Risen Christ to Jerusalem Jews and place the blame for his death squarely upon their blind leaders. (2:23-24; 3:13-15; 4:10; 5:27-32; 7:51 ff.) It is no wonder we read that, "the people magnified them; and believers were the more added to the Lord." (5:13-14.) God honored their courage.

In Moving Out Upon Many Untried Ways

Judaism was an ancient religion and the passing centuries had seen changes come slowly. Always and everywhere the Gentile was without the pale and beyond the promises of Israel.

But see how these first Christians dared to break precedent. What they had was the leading of the Holy Spirit and they believed that was enough. The living of believers was at stake and they proceeded at once to set up a new sort of economy. It was probably unlike anything they had seen before, but it worked and that was what concerned them at the moment. They needed help in handling funds and the office of deacon was established without delay. Philip went to Samaria and "proclaimed unto them the Christ." Peter and John went up from Jerusalem to investigate this hitherto unheard-of thing, and when they saw the fruit of the Spirit among these despised people the record says they "preached the gospel to many villages of the Samaritans." Philip broke over national and racial lines to preach Jesus to an Ethiopian. Peter visited and preached in the home of Cornelius, a soldier from the despised Roman legions, and after that there was no turning back. These men had dared to break out of the old shell of Judaism, and the gospel was on its way across the whole world.

In Challenging the Entrenched Paganism of Rome

Rome had been able to conquer and she understood how to govern. She had always been kind to the gods of her conquered peoples. Instead of forbidding their worship and further embittering the lands she overran, Rome had adopted the policy of taking the gods into her pantheon. Many of her shrines to heathen deities were ancient and honored. The Delphian Oracle had a thousand years of history behind it and was famous throughout the Roman world. Crowning all her pantheon, Rome had, by New Testament times, deified the Emperor and her only religious requirement seems to have been that all should reverence him as supreme.

Now the early Christians faced this ancient and entrenched system of paganism and with *none* of it would they compromise. Those gods of Rome are gone and their very names have been forgotten now for more than a thousand years. Professor T. R. Glover in his *The Jesus of History* asks *how* that almost unbelievable thing ever came to pass and he answers his own question by saying that the Christians of that early church *out-thought, out-lived,* and *out-died* the pagans. From the very start they boldly challenged Rome's entrenched paganism, and their boldness finally won the day.

THE PAULINE LETTERS

ROMANS through PHILEMON

PAUL LESLIE GARBER

THE PAULINE LETTERS

THE PAULINE LETTERS

"Our beloved brother Paul ... wrote unto you ... in all his epistles ... some things hard to be understood ..."—II Peter 3:15-16.

What do Christians believe? What is the Christian life? When answers to these questions have been attempted, men have turned for guidance to Paul's writings more frequently perhaps than to any others save the four Gospels.

In five springtimes in Christian history, when the world has been blessed with new spiritual life, the first awakenings were prompted by the letters of Paul.

1. When the Epistles of Paul were originally collected, "published," and circulated, positive and clear answers were given to problems common to Gentile converts, answers from a forceful missionary with full apostolic authority. Paul's convictions colored what men thought of Christian faith and practice; his enthusiasm so aroused them that in less than three centuries the whole Roman world knew the life-changing Christ.

2. By A.D. 386 a winter of troubles, sin, and world-weariness had settled over the Empire and had all but stifled the life of the church. One sentence from the letter to the Romans, "Put ye on the Lord Jesus Christ, and make not provision for the flesh, to fulfil the lusts thereof" (13:14), was casually read by young Augustine. That sentence, never to be forgotten, incited in him new life in Christ which came to be light and life to a dark and dying world.

3. The Reformation was a renaissance of Christian vitality. Luther's "salvation by faith alone," and Calvin's "divine sovereignty," and much else in classical Protestantism reflect the Reformers' minute study of Paul's thought.

4. Two hundred years later the English Evangelical Awakening began when John Wesley at Aldersgate Chapel heard a reading

from Luther's *Preface to . . . Romans* and felt his "heart strangely warmed." Paul again.

5. In our time the influence of Karl Barth has been extensive. It is interesting that Barth first became known in this country largely through commentaries on two of Paul's letters, Romans and I Corinthians.

Our churches mark major events in each individual's life with special ceremonies; the language used on such occasions echoes Paul's phrases. At the baptism of infants we use, " a sign and seal of the remission of sins." In the marriage service there is a reflection of Paul's daring parallel, "Husbands, love your wives, even as Christ also loved the church, and gave himself up for it." In the funeral service our full New Testament statement of the Christian belief in the resurrection of the body is given in I Corinthians 15. Without Paul's record of the words of the institution of the Holy Supper of our Lord Jesus Christ, our knowledge of what transpired in the upper room on "the night in which he was betrayed" would be meager indeed.

What do Christians believe? What is the Christian life? No one can understand the answers, past or present, given to these questions without knowledge of the letters of Paul. Who, for example, would dare explain to a non-Christian the characteristics of Christian love without reference to I Corinthians 13?

Some of the Epistles were written with meticulous care, careful choice of words, and balancing of phrase with phrase, as in I Corinthians 13 and 15. But on the whole Paul's style is broken and rough. He was usually pioneering in the thoughts expressed. His words were dictated under emotional strain and with eagerness to get the message to his readers. The results make difficult reading for us. In Romans 1:8 and 3:2 "firstly" appears without a "secondly." "Going off on a word," a series of thoughts parenthetical to his main point, is characteristic of Paul's writing. Romans 1:1-7 is an inserted discourse on the word "gospel." Paul's sentences and paragraphs often end in ways surprisingly different from those anticipated at the beginning.

The modern reader needs also to be acquainted with several traits of Paul's thinking. One of these is his tendency to treat great truths by personification. Sin, for example, Paul thinks of as entering the world, being stimulated into action, establishing dominion over men and mastering them. Death, too, reigns, has dominion, and at last is to be swallowed up. Closely related to this kind of thinking is the Apostle's fondness for parallels—Gentile and Jew, life and death, Adam and Christ, the natural and the supernatural. Many of Paul's expositions are organized around parallels of this kind. These usages reflect Paul's early education when "as touching the law" he was a Pharisee. Paul's illustrations are largely from the sphere of legal relationships, and this tendency gives us many references to marriage, divorce, inheritance, property, personal rights. Adoption has been referred to as Paul's favorite figure. Little wonder it is that through the ages men trained to be lawyers like John Calvin and Martin Luther have found Paul, the ex-Pharisee, a congenial and stimulating advocate of Christ. Precise terminology, close-knit thinking, and comprehensive treatment give the Epistles a courtroom atmosphere of "the truth, the whole truth, and nothing but the truth."

As the Gospels of the New Testament are like the Law of the Old Testament, so the Epistles are like the Prophets. The prophets directed their "word of the Lord" to their own contemporaries and their messages had to do with specific problems which were of first importance in those days. The Epistle writers, too, had a word of God for particular individuals who in their circumstances were confronted with problems on the solution of which the salvation of souls depended. The modern reader needs to be well aware of those immediate circumstances which led to the writing of any given Epistle. This conviction has determined the large place devoted in the following studies to background.

The prophets, however, rarely employed the letter-form, whereas perhaps all but six of the New Testament books are real letters, originally written in the course of ordinary correspondence. The "baptism" of the letter form into its sacred use was at the hand of Paul.

The student of Paul's letters deals with writings which more than once have turned the world upside down. The style is not an easy one and Paul's ways of expressing himself often seem strange. It is to be remembered, however, that Paul wrote for ordinary people of his day to understand, and any ordinary reader today can discover at least his answers to the questions, What do Christians believe? and, What is the Christian life? This, after all, is what Paul intended, and what we need.

An Outline for Study

The importance of Paul's letters.
>   Past: the five springtimes.
>   >   (1) The First Century.
>   >   (2) Augustine.
>   >   (3) The Reformation.
>   >   (4) The English Evangelical Awakening.
>   >   (5) Barth.
>   Present: Paul in church life.
>   >   Baptism—Romans 4:11.
>   >   Marriage—Ephesians 5:25.
>   >   Funerals—I Corinthians 15.
>   >   The Lord's Supper—I Corinthians 11:23 ff.
>   >   Love—I Corinthians 13.
Difficulties for the modern reader.
>   Paul's writing style.
>   Paul's traits of thinking.
>   >   the use of personification.
>   >   the use of parallels.
>   >   his fondness for "legalisms."
The Epistles as real letters.
Comparison with the Old Testament prophets.
Paul wrote for ordinary people to understand.

II. THE LETTER TO THE ROMANS

"For I long to see you, that I may impart unto you some spiritual gift, to the end ye may be established . . ."—Romans 1:11.

The most complete statement of the Christian good news as the first century understood it is preserved in this letter. It is fortunate we have that statement from the pen of him who first brought Christianity to Europe.

Paul wrote from Corinth, a metropolitan center of the East. He had spent twenty years establishing Christian centers in Asia Minor and Greece. His hope was to give himself similarly to the West. This new effort he planned after a necessary trip to Jerusalem. As a preliminary step a letter was written to the established church in the capital city of the Empire to inform the Christians there of his plans, but more to clarify for them the gospel of Jesus Christ as he knew and taught it.

In the salutation Paul reveals a courteous but rather formal approach. He hastens to assure his readers, most of whom he has never seen, of his genuine, lasting, and personal interest in their growth as Christians.

The main theme of the Epistle and of Paul's preaching is declared in trumpetlike tones, "I am not ashamed of the gospel of Christ: for it is the power of God unto salvation to every one that believeth; to the Jew first, and also to the Greek." Only those are really alive who are good with the goodness that believers know. All others are dead, for death is the penalty God exacts for "ungodliness and unrighteousness."

This statement applies to the Jew and the non-Jew (Gentile) alike. Take first the case of the non-Jew. All any man can possibly discover about God the non-Jew can know from observing the way he made the world of nature. (1:20.) Another "witness" to God's requirements of righteousness is provided by conscience. (2:14-15.) But instead of becoming true worshipers and good people, the non-Jews have become devout in the worship of idols—images of men, of birds, of animals, and even of snakes. Because they entirely rejected God, God "gave them up to uncleanliness." This, Paul explains, is the reason for the dissolute and degrading physical passions so characteristic of Greek and Roman society. These Gentiles well know that God's justice demands immediate punishment for people who do these things, yet they persist in idolatry and immorality and even enjoy seeing others revel in wickedness. (1:32.)

Jews, on the other hand, who often condemn non-Jews as gross sinners, are equally guilty in the sight of God. (2:1.) The Jews proudly possess the Law in Scriptures and boast of their intimate acquaintance with God to the point of offering to instruct Gentiles in religion and morals, but in actions they reveal themselves to be "contentious"—rebels and doers of evil. Knowing the Scriptures will not save the lawbreakers. All law can do is to arouse a consciousness of sin and guilt. (3:20.) Hence all men, Jews and non-Jews, need some way of being made just in the sight of God.

The gospel's good news is that God has supplied the need of every man for a way to goodness and life. That way leads to goodness through faith in Jesus Christ. It is the way for all men, Jew and non-Jew alike. God displayed Christ dying as a sacrifice of reconciliation so that men might understand that with God there is at one and the same time forgiveness for sin and maintenance of his justice. (3:22-26.) Let no man, therefore, boast of deeds or race; neither counts with God, only faith matters. (3:27-30.)

In the Old Testament record of Abraham, God is revealed as saving a man by faith. (Ch. 4.) From the Christian's inner awareness of peace with God through Christ there is evidence that God saves by faith alone. All the evil Adam did in introducing sin into the world, Christ by his righteousness set right. Sin and its way of choking to death a man's inner vitality has had its day and is done. God's grace and mercy now rule to bring a resurrection of inner life to the one who believes. (Ch. 5.)

In chapters 6 and 7 Paul refutes three commonly offered objections to the gospel plan of salvation as he preached it to the Gentiles, that is, "salvation by faith alone." It was charged that Paul talked nonsense when he preached that for the man who believes in Christ, God offsets every sin with grace. The more sin therefore there is in this world, the more of the grace of God there will be also. That man serves God best who sins most! "God forbid," Paul replies. The believing Christian has no desire to sin. His connection with sin, like a disconnected electric light, is dead. He is alive only to godliness. The true Christian acts as one brought back to life from the death of sin, and out of gratitude he tries to be the kind of a person God wants him to be.

Paul's critics said also that the salvation by faith alone which he preached released Christians from all moral requirements. Not at all, Paul replies. The Christian is a freed slave of sin to become a slave of goodness, and this slavery pays wages not of death but of eternal life through our Lord Jesus Christ. (6:15-23.) The Christian is a widow of sin to be married again to God in order to be a constant and loyal wife to him. (7:1-6.)

At times Paul was accused of teaching that the Bible was false and the Ten Commandments were sinful. Certainly not! Paul asserts. The Scriptures and the Commandments are spiritual, "holy, and just, and good." But the man who in his own strength tries to live without breaking any of the commands of God finds himself baffled and thwarted. He wants to do right but always discovers that what he does is wrong. "Wretched man that I am! who shall deliver me . . . ?" Thank God! He delivers me through faith in Jesus Christ our Lord.

There is no power of evil, the Apostle concludes in the well-loved chapter 8, on earth, in heaven, or in the underworld that can bring any accusation before God against those who are "in Christ" by faith. God has put his life-giving Spirit in the believer and he is thereby freed from every destructive influence of sin and death. The Christian's moral obligation to God out of gratitude for this emancipation is to live as a loving and obedient child of the heavenly Father. The whole of God's created world has waited for such persons to appear upon the earth, and Christians themselves wait with hope until in the resurrection they are made completely that kind of persons. Meanwhile God's Spirit within makes the believer's unworthy praying acceptable before God. (8:26-27.) The Christian's confidence is that "to them that love God all things work together for good." (8:28.) "This is the victory . . . our faith." (I John 5:4.)

An Outline for the Study of Romans 1—8

Salutation. 1:1-7.
Paul's interest in the Roman Christians. 1:8-15.
The theme announced: Salvation by faith alone. 1:16-18.
    The universal need for the gospel. 1:19—3:20.
        Among the Gentiles. 1:19-32.

Among the Jews. 2:1—3:20.

What God has done to supply man's need—the work of Christ. 3:21-30.

Christ, the "propitiation." 3:25.

The common way of faith precludes all pride. 3:27-30.

Taught in the Old Testament. 4:1-25.

Experienced by the Christian. 5:1-11.

Illustrated: the Adam-Christ parallel. 5:12-21.

Note: verses 13-17 are parenthetical.

Three objections to "salvation by faith alone" refuted. 6:1—7:25.

1. That the doctrine doesn't make sense. 6:1-14.

Paul's answer. 6:2-14.

2. That the doctrine releases men from moral requirements. 6:15—7:6.

Paul's answer: the freed slave enslaved. 6:16-23.
the widow remarried. 7:1-6.

3. That the doctrine makes the Bible false. 7:7-25.

Paul's answer: On the contrary, when I attempt to live by the Law, I play false to the Bible. 7:22-23.

The gospel as emancipation from sin and death. 8:1-39.

The freedom. 8:1-11.

The obligation. 8:12-17.

The benefits. 8:18-39.

a new kind of being. 8:18-25.

prayers made acceptable. 8:26-27.

confidence unshakable. 8:28-39.

III. THE LETTER TO THE ROMANS

(Continued)

"I have great sorrow . . . in my heart . . . for . . . my kinsmen according to the flesh: who are Israelites . . ."—Romans 9:2-3.

During the early centuries of Christian history Judaism and Christianity were often engaged in bitter and heated conflict. No one knew both sides of the controversy so well as Paul. He was fully aware that many of his "kinsmen according to the flesh" regarded him as a renegade and a traitor; not a few were convinced that "it is not fit that he should live." (Acts 22:22.) Nevertheless the Apostle to the Gentiles could not forget his Hebrew ancestry. He could never deny his early-formed conviction that Israel was God's chosen instrument for the salvation of the world. That divine selection, it seemed to him, must be eternal and unchangeable; otherwise the righteous God would be fickle in his affections, and that was unthinkable.

The question Paul and every fair-minded Christian had to answer was this: How could God's people reject God's Son? The answer was of great practical importance, for it determined the attitude Christians should take toward Jews. Should Jews be shunned and avoided as enemies of God, or approached as worshipers of a common God needing only that fuller knowledge of him which comes by faith in Jesus Christ? Paul records his views on this matter in Romans 9—11.

"My heart's desire and supplication to God for Israel is for them, that they may be saved." (10:1.) Here is Paul's personal attitude. His desire is profound: "For I could wish that I myself were anathema from Christ," damned eternally, if that would help my brethren to be saved! (9:3.)

The argument in chapters 9—11 is close-knit and detailed. Paul affirms the truth of Scripture that to "Israel" God gave all the blessings the Jews claim, and Christ too. But not all Hebrews by blood are called to be children of God; only those whom God chooses to love. Hence not all Jewry has been or will immediately be Christian converts. Does this mean that God has repudiated his people? Not at all. It means only that now the "seven thousand men, who have not bowed the knee to Baal," the chosen remnant, have believed or will believe and be saved. The rest are "blinded" and deaf for the time being. The secret or "mystery" about the Jews is that although now a part of God's chosen people have rejected him, when all he has chosen from the Gentiles have been received, then "all Israel shall be saved" for God does not give gifts and extend calls and then take them back. (11:25-26.) How wonderful are his ways!

Gratitude for God's mercies in providing salvation by faith in Christ moves the Christian to efforts of goodness. To be transformed into a person who pleases God is like putting one's body on some sacrificial altar of thanksgiving. (12:1-2.) These statements introduce Paul's directives of Christian ethics in 12:1—15:13. Paul's experiences in evangelizing the Corinthian Gentiles are reflected here.

Christian fellowship through deference of one to the other is of prime importance; fellowship makes the church one and an extension in the world of Christ's redeeming ministry. The love Christians bear one another must be blameless, revealing itself in mutual affection and happiness, in hope, patience, and prayer, and in Christ's radically different treatment of persecutors and enemies. "Be not overcome of evil, but overcome evil with good." (12:21.)

Civil authorities are God's agents of blessing to those who want to be good. Christians should obey them, therefore, and pay taxes. The coming "day of the Lord" should make Christians be more rather than less honest, sober, and loving. (Ch. 13.)

One can afford to go the second mile with the overscrupulous or "weak in the faith." They are Christ's servants and your brothers. While recognizing that these matters of diet or days of observance do not make up the essentials of the Kingdom of God, we have no business criticizing our brothers and Christ's servants for their scruples. (Ch. 14.)

In chapter 15 Paul returns to the subject of unity of spirit and harmony among Christians. From 15:14 to the closing the Epistle grows more personal. I am proud of what Christ has accomplished through me, the writer seems to be saying, for I have preached the gospel from Jerusalem all the way to Illyricum (roughly, modern Yugoslavia). When I go to Spain, I want to visit you. Just now I am going to Jerusalem with a contribution from the Greeks. When that is finished, I will come to you. Pray that I escape the Jewish enemies of Christianity in Judea and that what we take to Jerusalem may be accepted. Thus I can come to you with joy.

Phoebe, who may have carried this letter from Corinth to Rome, is introduced and commended at the beginning of the closing chapter.* Note the names of women in the Roman church. From these Greek, Roman, and Jewish names one discovers the international and interracial makeup of the church. Paul records the names of his companions in the greetings, even allowing his secretary to add a sentence of his own.

A brief benediction and a longer doxology close the Epistle. In the latter is a partial summary of the gospel according to Paul. Significantly it ends, "To the only wise God, through Jesus Christ, to whom be glory for ever. Amen.

An Outline for the Study of Romans 9—16

With reference to the Jews. 9:1—11:36.
 God promised blessings to "Israel" (9:4-5),
  but not to all Hebrews. 9:6-18.
 He, as Sovereign, has the right to choose. 9:19-29.
 The Jews' rejection due to the refusal of a way of salvation taught in their own Scriptures. 9:30—10:21.
 A remnant has believed. 11:1-10.
 All ultimately will be converted. 11:11-32.
  Note: Parenthetical warning for Gentile converts. 11:13-24.
 The doxology. 11:33-36.
Exhortation to Christian living. 12:1—15:13.
 The motive: gratitude for salvation by faith. 12:1-2.
 United in the church's life and work. 12:3-8.
 Practicing irreproachable mutual love. 12:9-21.
 Christians are good citizens. 13:1-10.
 Honesty and sobriety parts of Christian love. 13:11-14.
 Concerning the overscrupulous. 14:1-23.
 Harmony through mutual forbearance. 15:1-13.
Personal messages and salutations. 15:14—16:27.
 Paul's plans: 15:14-33.
 Greetings. 16:1-23.
 Benediction and doxology. 16:24-27

---

*It is held by some that 15:33—16:23 is not a part of the original Epistle to the Romans but rather a letter of Paul for another purpose. The reasons for and against this view are discussed in the Westminster Bible dictionary, p. 519.

IV. THE LETTERS TO THE CORINTHIANS

"Christ the power of God, and the wisdom of God."—I Corinthians 1:24.

If the gospel could win in pagan Corinth, it could win anywhere. That victory seemed improbable, yet by the "power of God" the gospel carried the day—but only after a contest in which it was severely tried.

Corinth was a city of two ports. Much world commerce passed through Corinth. Sailors with shore leave and wages to spend crowded her streets. The temple of Venus, overshadowing the city, symbolized the character of its life. As the people's religion, so the citizens became. No form of lewdness and vice was lacking in this Roman Shanghai.

The gospel began in Corinth in a home, in a shop, in the market place, and in the synagogue. For a period of eighteen months with his friends, Priscilla and Aquila, and later with Timothy and Silas (II Cor. 1:19), Paul preached "Jesus Christ, and him crucified" plainly and simply. He claimed the Lord's promise and proved it, "I have much people in this city." (Acts 18:10.)

Probably two or more years passed after Paul left Corinth before he had his first word of church conditions there. He had just arrived in Ephesus when news came that the Corinthians were drifting back into pagan ways. One member of the church was living in open adultery with his father's widow, a stepmother. This was a crime under Roman law yet the Corinthian church winked at it. Paul immediately dispatched a stern letter advising the Corinthians not to associate with professing Christians who persist in unrepented sex immorality. (I Cor. 5:9.) This "previous" letter has been lost unless, as some think, a fragment is preserved in II Corinthians 6:14—7:1.

When it was learned in Corinth that their former pastor was in Ephesus, two days sailing time away, several like Chloe visited him. Then a letter came from the church (the only letter we know Paul ever received) and it stated many questions troubling the Corinthian

Christians. Paul's reply is our I Corinthians; its arrangement is topical.

After congratulating his readers on their growth as Christians, Paul singles out as the church's most serious defect its factions, petty groupings claiming as rival Christian heroes, leaders, and examples Paul, Apollos, Peter, and Christ. The correction to factionalism is the realization that God is the sole source of spiritual life and power, that Christ is the only crucified and risen Saviour, and that all Christians are therefore on an equality since all are equally dependent. Paul, Apollos, and Peter are just stewards of God.

In chapters 5 and 6 Paul insists on the necessity of discipline exercised by the church over the morality of its members. Christians who take disagreements with fellow Christians into civil law courts demonstrate the need for more discipline by the church. That a Christian should allow his physical passion to run away with him shows how little he prizes his body which is, Paul asserts, "a temple of the Holy Spirit which is in you." Your body is not yours; God has bought it and paid for it, and your use of it should honor its Owner.

Chapter 7 deals with this question: in view of the present distress (evil days preceding the return of Christ), should people marry?

In chapter 8 Paul takes up another question: where should Christians buy meat? This innocent query probably did not bother the average Corinthian Christian, but it was a serious moral issue for the more sensitive members of the church. Pagan religious ritual centered largely in animal sacrifice. The blood was poured out before the idols; the meat of the animals was afterward offered for sale. Since only the fattest, choicest animals were used, the temple markets sold the best cuts of meat available. Would eating meat once used in idol worship be disloyal to Christ? Was it right to patronize a pagan meat market and so keep it in the business? For some modern Christians a parallel moral issue is involved in buying groceries from a store which also sells beverage alcohol.

Paul is painstaking in his answer, 8:1—11:1. His basic principle, balancing freedom with consideration for the scruples of others, is given in 10:23-24. In chapter 9 he refers to his foregoing a preacher's right to financial support. Sometimes, he says in effect, it is nobler to voluntarily relinquish one's rights than to insist upon them.

The 13th chapter of I Corinthians is a part of the Apostle's instruction on the nature of true Christian worship, Paul's effort to bring order out of the chaotic conditions reported to exist in Corinthian church services. The touchstone for every part of services worthy of the Lord is this: "Let all things be done unto edifying." (14:26.) Everything done must be for the good of all present.

In light of this principle Paul stated that women ought to wear something on their heads in church. Only prostitutes appeared in Corinthian public places bareheaded. The Lord's house is not a banquet hall, nor is the Lord's Supper like a pagan god's communal meal, usually a drunken revel. At the Lord's Supper the Christian remembers in quiet, humble decency Jesus the crucified. Every worshiper has a place in the fellowship of praise. No one, not even apostles, has "better" spiritual talents; all have "the best gifts" when everyone follows the "more excellent way" of charity or love.

Certain aspects of the resurrection puzzled the Corinthians. Before they became Christians, the Greeks among them believed the soul could be immortal only as in some way it was released from the body. The Jews, however, had been taught that life could not exist apart from the body. Paul in chapter 15 insists that resurrection of the body is a necessary part of Christian faith. But, he explains, the resurrection body is not physical and adapted to earthly needs as our present bodies are. It is a "spiritual body," adjusted and adapted as wondrously to heavenly necessities.

The Apostle tells his Corinthian friends his missionary strategy, urging: "Watch ye, stand fast in the faith, quit you like men, be strong." Then he adds personal greetings and an autographed curse and blessing.

Would the gospel win or lose in Corinth? Paul could but admonish and counsel. That he had done. Now he must wait and pray.

An Outline for the Study of I Corinthians

Introduction. 1:1-9.
   Congratulations that you "come behind in no gift."
Factionalism. 1:10—4:21.
   Corrective: realization that all Christians are equal in their common
      dependence upon God as sole source of spiritual life and power
      and upon Christ as the only crucified and risen Saviour.
   Paul, Apollos, and Peter merely stewards together.
The necessity for church discipline. Chs. 5-6.
   The incest case. Ch. 5.
   Lawsuits. 6:1-11.
   Sex purity and self-control; God's ownership of the body. 6:12-20.
The expediency of marriage. Ch. 7.
   Paul's rule "in all churches," 7:17, 20, 24, and his concession, 7:28.
Freedom and social responsibility. 8:1—11:1.
   The principle. 10:23-24.
   Illustrations:
      a. Meat once offered to idols. Ch. 8.
      b. Paul's right to financial support. Ch. 9.
      c. Association with pagans. 10:1—1:1.
The conduct of Christian worship. 11:2—14:40.
   Women's hats. 11:2-16.
   The Lord's Supper. 11:17-34.
   The gift of tongues. Ch. 12.
   The test is charity or love. (ch. 13),
      which means decency and order (ch. 14).
The Resurrection. Ch. 15.
   The Greek and Jewish preconceptions.
   Paul's concept, a "spiritual body."
Conclusion. Ch. 16
   Paul's missionary strategy. 16:1-14.
      The offering. 16:1-4.
      Provision for spiritual oversight. 16:5-14.
   Personal matters. 16:15-20.
   Farewell. 16:21-24

V. THE LETTERS TO THE CORINTHIANS

(Continued)

"God was in Christ reconciling the world unto himself . . ."
—II Corinthians 5:19.

II Corinthians, like I Corinthians, reveals the gospel's difficulties in evangelizing Gentiles. It is, however, less logical and more intensely emotional. It may be thought of as three almost unrelated parts.

Paul's sharp rebuke of the Corinthian factional loyalties seems to have resulted in turning nearly the whole church against him. He may then have made a visit to Corinth. We know he wrote a "severe" or "sorrowful" letter. This was delivered by Titus and contained the sort of impassioned defense of Paul's apostolic authority we find in II Corinthians, chapters 10-13. The whole conflict distressed Paul "insomuch that we despaired even of life." (II Cor. 1:8.) In this depressed spirit he traveled from Ephesus to Troas and on to Philippi; neither old friends nor opportunities for new mission enterprises afforded him any comfort. But then Titus reached Paul with unbelievably good news. The crisis was passed; Paul's authority had been recognized, and discipline on the basis of his instructions had begun in the church. With joyous relief Paul wrote laying bare his heart and its feelings, cautioning them not to be too severe with their punishment of erring Christians, promising a visit to them soon and explaining at some length (II Cor., chs. 8—9) the collection mentioned in I Corinthians 16:1-4.

Part One. II Corinthians 1—7. Paul reflects on the trouble he experienced in Ephesus and Troas (Asia) when he was so anxious about conditions in Corinth. He sees in it a divine purpose to make him trust God rather than himself. Church censure, he counsels, is to be exercised in moderation and with due regard for the penitent's welfare.

In 2:12—7:16 Paul compares his reconciliation with the Corinthians to God's reconciliation to the world. The Apostle seems to have written hurriedly and emotionally; this makes reading difficult. The heart of the passage is 5:16—6:1, 3; 7:9-10.

Part Two. Chapters 8—9. In encouraging the Corinthians to take a generous share in the collection for needy Christians, Paul formulates certain sound principles of stewardship. (See the outline.)

Part Three. Chapters 10—13 consist of a heated but deliberate defense by Paul of his ministry. He points out criticisms made of him. Note the references in the outline. Put the charges of Paul's critics in your own words and see how keenly the Apostle replies. 11:16—12:13.

This will be my third visit to you, and when I come I will spare nobody. I don't want to "use sharpness" of authority against you, so "be perfected . . . live in peace." 12:14—13:14.

Corinth is a city of small significance today. For many years after the first century the Corinthian church had great influence in Christendom. But more significant than anything that church ever was or did are the letters the Apostle Paul wrote to it.

An Outline for the Study of II Corinthians

Part One. Chapters 1—7.
Salutation. 1:1-2.
The trouble in Asia. 1:3-11.
Designed to make Paul trust God alone.
Charges against him refuted. 1:12—2:4.
Counsel regarding church discipline. 2:5-11.
To be moderate and for the penitent's welfare.
Comparsion: Paul's reconciliation with the Corinthians and God's reconciliation with the world in Christ. 2:12—7:16.
Heart of the passage: 5:16—6:1, 3; 7:9-10.

Part Two. Chapters 8—9.
Regarding the collection for Jerusalem.
Basic principles of Christian stewardship:
8:3-5
8:9
8:12
8:20
9:7
9:12

Part Three. Chapters 10—13.
A heated defense against the Corinthian critics, who said:
He's bold when away, but unimpressive in person. 10:1-2, 10.
He's in the ministry for fleshly pleasure. 10:3.
He boasts too much. 10:8.
He's a contemptible speaker. 10:10.
He doesn't charge anything. 11:7.
He's a fool! 11:16.
Plea:
"Be perfected . . . live in peace."—13:11-14.

VI. THE LETTER TO THE GALATIANS

"For freedom did Christ set us free: stand fast therefore."—
(Galatians 5:1.)

The Christian faith is free from all alliances with nations and in-
stitutions. By virtue of its uniqueness it is independent of every other
religion. Such a statement is commonplace in the twentieth century.
Independence and universality were won in the first century, however, in a bitterly contested struggle. The letter to the Galatians made
a noteworthy contribution in that effort and remains today the
Magna Charta of Christian liberty.

Those addressed, whether residents of Galatia proper or of the
Roman province (see Westminster Bible dictionary, p. 190, "Galatia"). were emigrants from Gaul (modern France) some 350 years
before Paul wrote. Their mixed blood and their volatile tempera-
ments made them susceptible to sects and cults. Paul had been with
the Galatians more than once; the first time, he says, they "received
me as an angel of God." (4:14.) Afterward with equal ease they
entertained "Judaizers" from Jerusalem and yielded to their persua-
sion without considering perhaps how this might contradict their
previous Christian commitment under Paul.

When word of this reached the Apostle, he dictated to them a
letter in which he exercised the whole range of his emotional capacity, from rebuke and sarcasm to painful earnestness and pathetic

pleading. Through the letter, moreover, a closely reasoned argument runs in which is the gist of Paul's gospel to the Gentiles—Romans in miniature.

Who were these "Judaizers"? They were Christians who, guided by the Old Testament as the Word of God, the example of Jesus and his disciples, and the practices of the Jerusalem church, obeyed the Law of Moses and hence circumcized, carried out dietary purity, and upheld all other Jewish ritualistic procedure. Every "first class" Christian, they urged, must do likewise. They seemed to have powerful authorities on their side of the argument—the Bible, Jesus, the apostles, and the mother church. What they overlooked were the clear evidences of the Holy Spirit's leading, such as Philip's success with the Samaritans (Acts 8:4-17), the conversion of the Ethiopian eunuch (Acts 8:27-39), the conversion of Cornelius (Acts 10:1—11:18), and the response among the Gentiles to the missionary efforts of Barnabas and Paul. The effect of their teaching was to keep Christianity a sect within Judaism, religiously, and thereby to limit the possibility of being Christian to those who were Jews by birth or by legal adoption.

Against the Judaizers, their principles and their policies, Paul was prepared to stand until death if need be. Plainly his whole mission to the Gentile world was in jeopardy. He wrote sharply, boldly, and feelingly. His letter was to stir Martin Luther to announce the principles of the Protestant Reformation. Paul, too, knew when to say, "Here I stand, I can do no other. God help me."

One of the charges the Judaizers made against Paul was that he was not a true apostle; he had never seen Jesus. Usually Paul graciously began his letters with thanksgiving and courteous appreciation of his readers. To the Galatians he boldly stated, "Paul, an apostle"— not an apostle of human origin or motives but one appointed by Jesus Christ and God the Father. I am shocked and surprised at how easily you have been alienated from me and won to a different gospel. There is no such thing, and anyone who preaches that there is, if I said so or an angel from heaven say so, a curse upon him! Again I say, "let him be accursed." Your new Judaizing friends say I, Paul, preach a human gospel designed to please human fancies—does this sound like it?

On this same high pitch of excitement the Apostle goes on in 1:11
—2:21 to review sketchily his career as a Christian in order to show
that his authority stems directly from the Damascus road experience
and Christ himself.

"O foolish Galatians, who did bewitch you," when you had Jesus
Christ crucified right before your eyes? This pitiful cry begins the
exposition of salvation by faith alone given in chapter 3. He appeals
to their own Christian experience as proof. He finds the doctrine
taught in Scripture: Abraham was saved by faith before there was
any Law. He discusses the nature of Law as a means of making men
good and concludes that any code of behavior has the value first of
a discipline and secondly of being the means of showing a man the
need of the Saviour. It is our "tutor to bring us unto Christ" (3:24);
it cannot save. There follow three further illustrations in chapter 4.

"For freedom did Christ set us free: stand fast therefore, and be
not entangled again in a yoke of bondage." (5:1.) Paul's exhortation
is perfectly plain—you were called to freedom, you were getting
along so well. Prize your freedom but don't turn it into license.
Live by the law of love and walk in the Spirit, and the fruit of the
Spirit will be yours.

With his own hand and large black letters such as a sign painter
might use, Paul writes 6:11-18 to reassert that no external rite, ceremony, or distinction, no proud badge of color, class, or nation, is of
any importance to a Christian. All that matters is that he, as each of
Christ's, is a "new creature." This is penned, as someone has said,
with all the bold daring that characterized John Hancock when he
signed the Declaration of Independence.

The Galatian churches may have disappeared from Christendom
with scarcely a trace, but as long as the Christian faith is proclaimed
a free and universal way of salvation to all, those to whom Paul once
wrote this letter will still be known.

An Outline for the Study of Galatians

Greetings. 1:1-5.
Paul's surprise expressed. 1:6-9.
   (an aside for the Judaizers' benefit. 1:10-12)

Paul traces the line of his apostolic authority from Christ. 1:13—2:21.
Proof of the validity of salvation by faith alone. 3:1-29.
  By their own Christian experience. 3:1-5.
  From Scripture: Abraham. 3:6-9.
  From the nature of law. 3:10-18.
    and its values. 3:19-24.
    and its weakness. 3:25-29.
Salvation by faith *illustrated*. 4:1-31.
  The analogy of sonship and its privileges. 4:1-11.
  They are in danger of returning to bondage. 4:8-11.
  The personal relation of Paul and the Galatians. 4:12-20.
  The allegory of Hagar and Sarah and their sons. 4:21-31.
The *exhortation:* "For freedom did Christ set us free: stand fast therefore." 5:1.
Prize freedom by living in love and by the Spirit. 5:2—6:10.
Paul's autograph. 6:11-18.
  All that matters is that a man is a new creature, freed from badges of color, class, and nation.

VII. THE LETTER TO THE EPHESIANS

"That Christ may dwell in your hearts through faith."—Ephesians 3:17.

The longest and perhaps most successful period of Paul's ministry was spent at Ephesus, capital of the province of Asia, its largest city and its most important center, commercially, politically, and religiously. For three years the Apostle labored there in synagogue, lecture hall, market place, and home to make Christ known in the cult-center of Diana. The dramatic highlights of those busy times are recorded in Acts, chapters 18 and 19.

A primary characteristic in Paul was his capacity for friendship. In each community he visited, he discovered those who became his life-long friends in Christ. Those he mentions by name in his Epistles make up an astonishingly large number. Many of these Paul must have known first in Ephesus.

It is surprising then to discover that the letter which claims to be

from Paul to the Christians at Ephesus contains not one line of greeting to any individuals, and it is still more curious that Paul should
write to the Ephesians in an impersonal and rather formal fashion,
as though they were not well acquainted. See 1:15 and 3:2. It has
been suggested that our present Ephesians is a circular letter to all the
churches of Asia and that in the first collection of Paul's letters it was
called "To the Ephesians" due to the prominence of the city and the
church. (See article, "Ephesians," in the Westminster Bible dictionary.)

So understood, the Epistle may be considered as a written sermon
sent by Paul to his spiritual children and grandchildren in the Christian churches in Asia and dated from a prison house in Rome about
A.D. 62. From references and similarities of expression, Ephesians,
Colossians, Philippians, and Philemon seem to have been written at
about the same time and are often called Paul's Prison Epistles. Of
the group Ephesians is the most logical and least personal. If Romans is Paul's exposition of the Gospel from East to West, Ephesians
is his preaching of Christ from West to East.

The Epistle is directed to the "saints," or professing Christians,
who are "faithful in Christ Jesus." It is helpful to trace the Doxology
to each person of the Trinity in turn in 1:3-14. My prayer, writes
Paul, is that God will give you wisdom and knowledge to realize
how great God's power of salvation is: it is as great as that he demonstrated in raising Christ from the dead and setting him on his
right hand.

Most of Paul's readers had been religiously and morally pagan
before they became Christians. You, the Apostle states, were then
dead because of your worldliness and sins. God by grace made us
alive with Christ and saved us. Salvation is a gift, not earned; no
man can boast of deserving it. God made us what we are as saved
Christians; he created us in Christ Jesus new men to live the life of
goodness.

When you were pagans, the Jews used to call you Gentiles "un-
circumcised," their word for godless heathen, Paul explains (2:11);
you were then aliens and strangers to God and to his chosen people.
"But now in Christ Jesus" you have been brought near and united

with faithful Israel. By the cross Christ offered himself for the salvation of Jew and non-Jew and set aside salvation through Jewish rules and regulations. In the church of Christ one is not "far off" and another "nigh" to God; all have one Spirit and may approach by his aid to the Father. All have Christ. The church is one, a structure like a temple compactly built together, a Spirit-created dwelling for God.

God mercifully gave me by a special revelation, Paul explains, "the mystery of Christ." This mystery is that Gentiles by faith in Christ are to be fellow heirs with Jews, God's chosen people. They are to be one body together in the church, sharers of the same promises of God. (3:6.)

The exalted prayer of 3:14-21 is earnest and profound. Growing Christians should know what "breadth and length and height and depth" mean, should understand the humanly incomprehensible love Christ has, and should be "filled unto all the fulness of God." The thought of such heavenly privileges leads the Apostle to burst forth in a doxology. (3:20-21.)

The remainder of the Epistle is an extended exhortation to live every day worthy of the summons to be God's children.

The Christian life is radically different from pagan ways; in being Godlike it is something new in this world. This is the sum of Christian living: to be strong in godliness by the power of God's might and to be protected, by the armor he provides, from all assaults of the Devil. Notice the allegory Paul makes out of the Roman soldier's battle uniform and equipment. (6:10-17.) Dr. Goodspeed translates "watching thereunto in all perseverance" in 6:18, "Be on the alert."

Luther called Ephesians, "one of the noblest books in all the New Testament, which shows thee Christ and teaches thee everything . . . necessary and good for thee to know . . ." Another has referred to 4:1—6:18 as "the widest and fullest practical survey of the field of social relations to be found in one continuous passage in the New Testament."

An Outline for the Study of Ephesians

Salutation. 1:1-2.
Doxology. 1:3-14.

Father. 1:3-6. Son. 1:7-12. Holy Spirit. 1:13-14.

Prayer. 1:15-23.

Christ's pre-eminent relation to the church. 1:21-23.

Sin and death universal apart from Christ. 2:1-3.

    Note "the prince of the powers of the air" in 2:2.

    (See Dummelow, p. 962.)

Salvation is resurrection with Christ by God's mercy. 2:4-10.

Remember "before and after." 2:11-22.

    Before: Aliens and strangers. 2:11-12.

    After: Reconciled by the cross. 2:13-18.

        Fellow citizens. 2:19.

        A living temple. 2:20-22.

The "mystery" for which Paul was in prison. 3:1-13.

    The "wisdom of God." (Compare Colossians 1:26-27.)

Prayer. 3:14-21.

    For strength from the Holy Spirit and the indwelling Christ. 3:14-19.

    Doxology. 3:20-21.

Exhortation to worthy Christian living. 4:1—6:9.

    Summarized in one sentence. 4:1-3.

    What makes up worthy Christian living. 4:4-16; 4:32—5:2.

    What is contrary. 4:17-31; 5:3-18a.

    Specific directions. 5:18b—6:9.

The allegory of the soldier's battle equipment. 6:10-17.

A plea for spiritual support. 6:18-20.

Regarding Tychichus. 6:21-22. (See Colossians 4:7.)

Benediction. 6:23-24.

VIII. THE LETTER TO THE PHILIPPIANS

"Wherefore, my brethren beloved and longed for, my joy and crown, so stand fast in the Lord, my beloved."—Philippians 4:1.

No other writing so clearly reveals the genial and sympathetic Paul as does this letter. It began as gratitude for a gift sent by friends to a friend. As it stands, it contains mainly personal news and counsel from a pastor to his flock.

Philippi was an important city in Macedonia. It was named for the father of Alexander the Great and, because of its historical significance, had been made a Roman colony. This gave its citizens added privileges. Philippian citizenship was highly prized.

Paul added to the distinctions of Philippi. He made it the first city in Europe to hear the gospel of Christ. Paul's preaching began by a river where a group of pious women were accustomed to meet for prayer. Lydia, a native of Asia and a business woman, was the first convert. Others mentioned in Acts 16 included a spirit-possessed girl and Philippi's head jailer. An anti-Semitic mob, a beating, an earthquake, and a near-suicide punctuated the end of Paul's first visit to Philippi. His preaching bore fruit. Time and again, the Philippians sent messages of affection and gifts of money to Paul. His Philippian labors were to Paul as near pure joy as earth afforded him.

When he returned to Philippi five years later, he was heartsick over the church at Corinth. Here Titus brought good news and Paul, so greatly relieved, wrote II Corinthians. The following spring, after spending the winter in Corinth, Paul returned to Philippi to spend the Easter season with them. True friends they are with whom one wishes to be in times of trouble as well as in times of rejoicing. Such friends were the Philippian Christians to Paul.

The letter has no fixed plan, but the subject of Paul's thought is clear throughout. Paul's prayerful gratitude is for the tie that binds fellow Christians together in confidence and work; his petition is that the Philippians will keep on growing in knowledge and right living.

In 1:27 the word translated in the King James Version "conversation" is rendered by the revised versions "citizenship." Be citizens worthy of the gospel, Paul urges. This involves certain qualities, including steadfastness against non-Christian influences (your not being terrified by their attacks is a testimony against them but is to your credit), unity of Christians, and Christlike humility. It is interesting to observe that Paul's witness to the exaltation of Christ, 2:5-11, was written originally to illustrate true humility.

News from Rome includes a word about Timothy and a word about Epaphroditus. The latter may have been a wealthy Christian who could leave his business for a year or more to serve Paul's needs, or a skilled masseur or male nurse whom the Philippians paid and sent, or he may have been an humble volunteer from the congregation entrusted with money and gifts from the Philippian church who remained to do what he could. Here Paul pens for Epaphroditus a citation for distinguished Christian service.

Paul in chapter 3 warns against two developments endangering the Christian movement. First, legalism promoted by Christians who, like the Galatian Judaizers, insisted that the only "first class" Christians are those who obey the Law of Moses. Of equal danger is lawlessness. There are many "enemies of the cross of Christ" who profess Christianity but who actually worship their physical bodies and revel in shameful things.

In his personal word to specific friends at Philippi, Paul bubbles over with affection. Euodia and Syntyche, two of the church women, are cautioned to work together in harmony, and an unidentified "true yokefellow," perhaps Epaphroditus, is to help them.

"Rejoice ... again I will say, Rejoice." The man who dictated these words was a prisoner, fettered to a Roman guard, and possibly nearing the end of his life's work. He possessed all the ingredients for despondency, but his words here (4:4-20) reveal the discipline of healthy Christian thinking. Think on things true, honest, just, pure, lovely, and of good report, and do what you have learned from me; then God and his peace will be with you.

The original purpose of the letter is almost the last topic treated. The Apostle expresses his gratitude for the Philippians' remembrances and gives a profound and priceless lesson. "I have learned" how to have and how not to have. "I can do all things in him" who gives me strength.

"For to me to live is Christ," Paul confessed to the Philippians. This letter itself is a witness to the truth of his assertion.

An Outline for the Study of Philippians

Salutation. 1.1-2.
(Earliest New Testament reference to "bishops," or elders, "and deacons.")
Gratitude. 1:3-11.
Prayer. 1:9-11.

Imprisoned and oppressed. 1:12-26.
  In face of death. 1:21-26.
Being citizens worthy of the Kingdom. 1:27—2:18. (Compare 3:20.)
  Steadfast. 1:27-30.
  United. 2:1-4.
  Humble-minded like Christ. 2:5-11.
  Serious and earnest. 2:12-18.
News from Rome. 2:19-30.
  Timothy. 2:19-24.
  Epaphroditus. 2:25-30.
Warnings. 3:1-21.
  Against legalism. 3:2-16.
  Against lawlessness. 3:17-21.
Regarding Paul's friends at Philippi. 4:1-3.
Final admonitions. 4:4-9.
Thanks for the gift. 4:10-20.
Greetings. 4:21-22.
Benediction. 4:23.

IX. THE LETTER TO THE COLOSSIANS

"... that no one may delude you with persuasiveness of speech."
—Colossians 2:4.

Does a man need more than Jesus to be saved? To answer this question Paul wrote Colossians. An unauthorized teaching being promoted among these people urged additions to the Pauline salvation by faith alone, as being necessary for their certain and eternal redemption.

The exact content of this teaching we know only by Paul's rebuttal to it. It seems to have been an effort to fit Jesus and his work as Saviour into pre-Christian, pagan religious conceptions. To relate the Christian faith and non-Christian religion is often a troublesome difficulty.

To those raised in the atmosphere of Greek religion the chasm between God and the material world was so vast that it could be bridged only by myriads of angelic beings. These were of varying degrees of godliness, some almost demon-like. Each part of the natural world had its guiding angel. Mere man was thought incapable of speaking face to face with the pure and ethereal Super-God, but he might approach angels. It was the angels, in any case, who actually determined the destinies of human individuals. Influence with "thrones," "dominions," "principalities," and "powers" was thought to be aided by the worshiper's denial of physical demands. By adoration and ascetic practices the worshiper's spirit was exalted and he was enabled to hold fellowship with angelic beings of increasingly higher rank and order. To Christian converts from this background, Jewish rites like circumcision and rigorous observances of feasts and fasts were much more reasonable than was Paul's simple doctrine of faith in Christ and a moral life in accordance with this profession.

About A.D. 62, when Paul was in prison at Rome, word concerning the rise of the heretical teaching at Colossae reached him through the report of Epaphras, a follower of Paul and missionary to the Colossians. For some reason Paul detained Epaphras, but he wrote a letter and sent it to the Colossian church by Tychicus, who perhaps also carried with him our letter to the Ephesians. Paul knew the church. Colossae was only 100 miles from Ephesus. Paul may have been the church's "grandfather" in Christ.

Colossae, Laodicea, and Hierapolis were adjacent cities of the Lycos River Valley in Asia Minor. Natives of this section had the reputation of being a volatile, emotional, and unreliable sort of people. More than two centuries before Paul wrote his letter, two thousand Jewish families had been imported from Babylonia in an effort to give the community a semblance of balance. This transplanting made Jewish thought well known in the Lycos Valley. Tendencies toward emotional excess and the influence of Jewish practices made the Colossians the more susceptible to those teachings Paul considered so dangerous to their church and to the whole Christian movement.

Paul's estimate has been proved correct many times over in Christian history. Whenever Christians allow themselves to be persuaded that they need something more than Jesus for their eternal salvation, Christianity is weakened and toned down. It seemed to the Colossians an intellectual, tolerant, and broad-minded thing for them as Christians to include in their religious thinking the angelic powers of pagan worship and to follow in their religious practices Jewish rites and ceremonies. The weakness of such "higher thought," Paul correctly insisted, is that it tends to make the Christian indifferent to that strenuous morality necessary to "a worthy walk" with Christ.

The Apostle's strategy against the subtle and insidious infiltration tactics of pseudo-intellectual and sophisticated theosophy and new thought is clear. It is defense by affirmation. Dr. Charles R. Erdman comments: "The best way to meet error is to emphasize truth."

For the Christian, all schemes of intermediary angels are condemned and all worship of angels, demons, or humans is prohibited by the gospel's one sufficiency, Christ. In his relation to God, to the created world, and to the church, Christ surpasses and excels all beings thought to mediate between God and man. He possesses all divine power, as he demonstrated when he reconciled to God all sinful things and men in earth and in heaven through his death on the cross. The most evident proof of Christ's pre-eminence, Paul asserts, lies in the Colossians' personal Christian experience. By him, and by him alone, you who were aliens and enemies toward God are reconciled to God, and presented in God's presence without blame or reproach.

Many pagan religious cults with which the Colossians were familiar, like fraternal orders today, had "mysteries" or "secrets" known only to initiated members. Christianity, too, has a "mystery," Paul insists, now known to Christian saints. It is this: Christ, the Pre-eminent One of all the universe, is within the Christian. Paul states his desire that the Colossians may have full assurance in this "mystery" so that they will be comforted in heart and united in love. Christ, he repeats, is the mystery of all mysteries, the secret of all secrets, "in whom are all the [so-called] treasures of wisdom and knowledge hidden."

Paul warns against the "persuasiveness of speech"—pseudo-philosophy, human traditions—which are sometimes used to beguile, to deceive, and to exploit. Your best defense against such pretenses is "as therefore ye received Christ Jesus the Lord, so walk in him."

Jesus Christ as Saviour is all any man needs. Let no man add to faith in him requirements for salvation concerning meats, drink, holidays, or feasts; these are relics of the past. Why will Christians become "subject . . . to ordinances," such as "Handle not, nor taste, nor touch . . ."? These make "a show of wisdom" but there is no honor in them; they are actually just a satisfaction of the flesh.

The guide to true Christian living is to seek heavenly ideals and fix your ambition on them alone. (3:1-17.)

Directions are given concerning the reading of this letter and of "the epistle from Laodicea." (4:16.) Was this the letter we know as Ephesians? (See article, "Laodicea," Westminster Bible dictionary.)

His bonds and Christ's grace are the two things Paul included in his autographed signature.

The letter to the Colossians is not easy for a modern reader. Paul wrote to combat a heresy about which we know little. He uses terms meaningful to the Colossians but difficult for us now to understand. Paul merely outlined his argument in writing. He depended on his personal emissary, Tychicus, to elaborate and illustrate each point verbally until the whole matter was perfectly clear.

This Epistle rendered a great service in its day, protecting the Colossian church and the Christian movement from many possible vagaries and delusions. The uniqueness of Christ, together with his demand that the Christian way be a radically ethical life, are the Epistle's trumpet calls. Both of these are necessary if contemporary Christians are to be kept from the sophisticated, pseudo-intellectual, pseudo-scientific, pseudo-Christian, and morally unprincipled sects and cults current in the urban centers of our land.

The word still stands: No man needs more than Jesus to be saved.

An Outline for the Study of Colossians

Salutation. 1:1-2.
Gratitude. 1:3-5a.
    (The hallmark of a Christian life—faith, hope, love. Compare I Thess. 1:2-3 and I Cor. 13:13.)
The true message of the gospel. 1:5b-12.
    Came through Epaphras. 1:6-8. Nothing more is needed. Paul prays

for their full knowledge and worthy Christian living. 1:9-12. Compare 2:6-7.

Pre-eminence of Christ in God's saving actions. 1:13-23.

Pre-existence—agency in creation—in preservation. 1:13-17.

Head of the church. 1:18.

Reconciler of the worlds. 1:19-20.

and of sinners. 1:21-23.

(Relation of Paul's imprisonment to the gospel. 1:24-25.)

Has a "mystery"—Christ in you, the hope of glory. 1:26—2:3.

Warning against false teachings. 2:4-23.

They are "persuasiveness of speech"—pseudo-philosophies. 2:4-5.

Best defense against them is a life in Christ. 2:6-7.

(Compare Ephesians 3:17.)

His pre-eminence as the fullness of God over all principalities and dominions. 2:8-10.

His is true circumcision. 2:11.

He raised you to life. 2:12-13.

He erased the record of sin. 2:14.

He exposed the pretensions of angelic beings. 2:15.

There is need for nothing more than Christ. 2:16-23. (Compare 2:6-10; 1:26—2:3.) Regulations—feasts—humiliations—visions—pseudo-wisdom—and human rules and regulations avail nothing.

True Christian living. 3:1-17.

Guided by ideals. 3:1-4.

Is as dead to bodily temptations. 3:5-8.

Acts truly, following the example of Christ. 3:9-10.

Knows no aristocracy. 3:11.

Symbolized as clothing, of which love is the finishing touch. 3:12-14.

(The test of Christian worship services. 3:15-17.)

Specific instructions. 3:18—4:1.

A plea for remembrance. 4:2-6.

Greetings and directives. 4:7-17.

Signature and blessing. 4:18.

X. THE LETTERS TO THE THESSALONIANS

"Prove all things; hold fast that which is good."—I Thessalonians 5:21.

Only the informed Christian can be "worthy of God," consecrated through and through. Some instruction can be given by word of mouth, but churches need also that which can "be read unto all the brethren." (I Thess. 5:27.) This conviction prompted these two brief letters, probably the earliest of Paul's writings the Holy Spirit has saved for us. The necessity of Christian education for worthy Christian living was the basis for these letters, among the oldest known written Christian messages.

Not long after the Apostle arrived in Corinth the first time, he received word through Timothy about the group of Gentiles Paul had won for Christ at Thessalonica. Just a few months before, Paul had been in that great port city. He had spoken first in the Jewish synagogue and had "reasoned with them from the scriptures . . . that this Jesus, whom . . . I proclaim unto you, is Christ." (Acts 17:2-3.) A few Jews were convinced, but many Greeks, near proselytes to Judaism, immediately followed Paul.

Most of these new converts were without social prominence; they were folk whom Paul, the part-time tentmaker, could meet weekdays in the shops and market places. They had been partially instructed in the Jewish religion but they had no Christian writing, no hymns, no prayers, no discipline, and no record of the life and teaching of Jesus. All they had was what Paul and Silas—and later Timothy—had given them orally.

The Jews at this time were engaged in a vigorous Empire-wide program of winning the Gentiles to the Law of Moses. Some of the Thessalonian synagogue leaders, jealous over Paul's taking Greek "prospects" away from them, stirred up a mob on the pretext that the new faith was a revolutionary political movement in disguise.

The leading Thessalonian Christians were personally embarrassed by the riot; some had to go under bond before the civil authorities were satisfied. Paul, not wishing to cause further trouble, went away.

After he was gone, he realized how inadequate a foundation he had been able to lay in Thessalonica. Time and again he tried to go back, but "Satan hindered us." Timothy could be sent back; the authorities would not recognize him as a Christian. He was sent, and time hung heavy for Paul until Timothy should return.

Timothy reported to Paul at Corinth. There were difficulties of Christian thought and action with which the Thessalonian followers needed help, but, on the whole, conditions there were good. They had met persecution without too much faltering, and they were earnestly striving the best they knew how to live in accordance with their new-found faith. The gratitude and relief Paul experienced is fully expressed in the first of the Thessalonian letters. See how many words of affection and regard are in the first three chapters of I Thessalonians.

How to live worthily as a Christian becomes the subject of Paul's instruction in chapters 4 and 5. His first word is that a Christian abstains from sexual immorality, for God has called us to purity. Secondly, the Christian life is one of mutual love and orderliness. Concerning dead believers, Christians ought not to sorrow; the dead are "asleep in Jesus" and will be given priority in all the glories of the resurrection.

Paul had made mention during his preaching in Thessalonica of "the day of the Lord" but he had not had time to make the matter clear. (See Westminster Bible dictionary article, "Day of the Lord.") Some of these half-instructed folks in the church were saying, "If the Lord is coming soon, why should we work to save up for old age?" Paul writes that no believer knows "the times and the seasons." Let us therefore watch, be sober, and strengthen one another. Christians are to respect the recognized church officers, at the same time silencing no one who may claim to be led by the Holy Spirit. Rather, "prove all things; hold fast that which is good."

A few months or perhaps weeks later Paul heard that conditions in Thessalonica had become worse. Many in the church had become convinced that "the day of the Lord" of which Paul had taught them had already come, beginning possibly in some place like Palestine, and that very soon its effects would be apparent in Thessalonica. This had resulted in a general letdown.

The first chapter of II Thessalonians, like that of I Thessalonians, reveals how deep was Paul's gratitude for the Christian faith and life he observed in the Thessalonians; they will be on the side of Christ when the day of the Lord comes. By no means has this event already taken place. Paul in the second chapter reminds his readers that the day of the Lord was to be preceded first by a general rebellion or apostasy and secondly by the appearance of one who is described as "the man of sin," "the son of perdition," and as one who "opposeth and exalteth himself against all that is called God, or that is worshipped." John called him "antichrist." (I John 2:18.) Since no widespread apostasy has taken place and no antichrist has appeared, Paul urges, the day of the Lord cannot have come.

With this assurance, Paul reasserts his previous exhortations: "Stand fast, and hold the traditions which ye have been taught, whether by word, or by epistle of ours," and "Be not weary in well-doing." This involves prayer, and living that is quiet and orderly, and an avoidance of those who live in idleness, treating such not as enemies but as erring brothers.*

The Thessalonian church became the asset to Christianity which Paul prayed it would be. In the ninth century, brothers went out from this church as missionaries to the Bohemians and the Moravians. From those people came the pre-Reformation martyr, John Hus, and many another leader to quicken the spiritual vitality of Christendom.

An Outline for the Study of I and II Thessalonians

I Thessalonians
>   Salutation. 1:1.
>   Thanksgiving. 1:2-10.
>   Paul's Thessalonian ministry recalled. 2:1-16.
>>   The manner of Paul's life. 2:1-12.
>>   How the gospel was received. 2:13-16.

---

* "If any will not work, neither let him eat." Did Captain John Smith who invoked this same regulation in the Virginia colony realize that it was first a Pauline command?

More recent history. 2:17—3:13.
  Paul's plans. 2:17-20.
  Timothy's visit. 3:1-5.
  Timothy's report and Paul's joy. 3:6-13.
Exhortation to lives pleasing to God. 4:1-12.
  Abstain from fornication—defrauding.
  Love—be quiet—work.
Concerning the dead. 4:13-18.
Concerning the day of the Lord. 5:1-11. (Compare II Thessalonians 2:1-7.)
Admonitions and benediction. 5:12-28.

II Thessalonians
  Salutation. 1:1-2.
  Thanksgiving. 1:3-10.
  Prayer. 1:11-12.
  Concerning the false rumor that the day of Christ had come. 2:1-17.
    Note "man of sin," 2:3.
    (See article, "Antichrist," Westminster Bible dictionary.)
  Exhortations. 3:1-16.
    Prayer—treatment for idlers—work.
  Paul's autograph and benediction. 3:17-18.

XI. THE LETTERS TO TIMOTHY

"Timothy, my beloved child . . ."—II Timothy 1:2.

I and II Timothy and Titus are "pastoral" because Paul wrote as pastor and discussed problems which are those of pastors.* I Timothy and Titus contain policies on church relations with social groups, on qualifications for church officers, on the conduct of worship, on the treatment of false teachers in the church—all matters of organization and discipline. Such problems developed in the latter part of the Apostolic Age and therefore the pastoral letters are possibly the latest New Testament writings, certainly the last of Paul's letters.

---

* The Pastoral Epistles are considered by many scholars to be expansions by later writers of fragments of genuine letters of Paul. For discussion of authorship see Dummelow's commentary.

More than a half-dozen times in the various Epistles Paul names Timothy as a fellow preacher, Christian worker, and slave of Jesus Christ. He reserves for Timothy the most intimate and affectionate words in his vocabulary.

It is impossible to reconstruct even a sketch of Timothy's life. He was chosen for difficult assignments, did the work quietly and well, and then disappeared with no word concerning his fate. Timothy, who was the son of a Greek father and a Jewish mother, Eunice, was a convert at Lystra. After Timothy was circumcised, he was added to Paul's band of traveling evangelists on the second missionary journey. He was with Paul at Troas when the "man of Macedonia" called out, "Come over . . . and help us" and, as the Epistle to the Philippians clearly implies, Timothy was with Paul there on the first visit and on at least two other occasions. It was Paul's plan that if his first Roman imprisonment ended in the death penalty Timothy should bear the sad news to Philippi. Such was the intimate relation between the Apostle and his understudy, the "father" and "son."

When I Timothy was written, Paul, who had probably been set free after his first trial at Rome, had placed Timothy at Ephesus as an apostolic deputy. This was a responsible post, particularly for a young man. A number of churches were associated with Ephesus. The "seven churches" of Revelation, as Sir William Ramsay has pointed out, were on a "circuit" beginning at Ephesus. Furthermore, at this time church life was becoming more complicated, with the necessity for organization, for rules regarding the selection of officers and the enforcement of church standards, and for policies related to various important aspects of congregational government. II Timothy is usually thought to have been written two or three years after I Timothy. Timothy was still at Ephesus. Paul's second letter contains no criticism of Timothy's work; its tone implies the Apostle's full satisfaction with the results of Timothy's labors. Higher praise no man could receive, for Paul was not easily pleased.

I Timothy consists of two divisions, chapters 1—3 and chapters 4—6. The first division deals with church policies.

The second division of I Timothy, chapters 4—6, is directed more personally to Timothy himself. Chapter 4 develops what Paul wrote in chapter 1 about false teachers. Timothy is counseled to take the positive approach in dealing with false doctrine, namely, to set a good example in conduct, to keep on proclaiming what he was led to believe was true, and to be critical of his own teaching lest it be touched with error.

An Outline for the Study of I Timothy

Salutation. 1:1-2.
False teachers. 1:3-20.
    Timothy's duty to warn. 1:3.
    The goal of teaching is "charity." 1:5.
Worship. 2:1-15.
    Prayer for all, including Nero. 2:1-4.
    Christ to be pre-eminent. 2:5-7.
    Men to worship without angry disputes (2:8) and women without
        fashion parades or presumption (2:9-15).
Church officers. 3:1-16.
False teachers. 4:1-16.
    Positive dealing with false doctrine. 4:6-7.
    Effectiveness of a good example. 4:12.
Treatment of various groups within the church. 5:1—6:19.
    Paul's zeal for the good name of Christian. 5:7, 14.
    Older and younger men. 5:1.
    Older and younger women. 5:2-16.
        Widows. 5:3-6, 8-16.
    Elders. 5:17-22.
    Slaves. 6:1-2.
    False teachers. 6:3-10.
    Personal advice to Timothy. 6:11-16.
    Rich. 6:17-19.
Parting plea to guard the truth with which Timothy has been entrusted and to avoid everything else that claims to be knowledge. 6:20-21.

The depth of Paul's personal affection for Timothy is plainly written into the opening sentences of II Timothy. The old prisoner's gratitude is based upon the confidence he has in Timothy's abilities and in his continuing to "be not ashamed" either of Christ's gospel or of Christ's prisoner, Paul. The man in chains bids the man who has none have courage!

An Outline for the Study of II Timothy

Salutation. 1:1-2.
Gratitude. 1:3-5.
Exhortations to faithfulness and endurance. 1:6—2:13.
  Necessity for courage. 1:6-12. (Compare 1:8 with 2:11.)
  Necessity for holding fast to the truth. 1:13-18.
  Necessity for being strong in Christ. 2:1-13.
    Commit the truth to faithful men. 2:2.
    Endure hardship. 2:3.
    Be single-minded as soldiers and as athletes. 2:4-5.
    Be diligent as a farmer who then is rewarded at harvest. 2:6.
    Be faithful to the teachings and example of Paul. 2:7-10.
      Paul is bound, God's word is not. 2:9.
    A Christian hymn or familiar saying. 2:11-13.
Warnings. 2:14—3:17.
  Against false teachers. 2:14-21.
  Against controversy. Only gentleness and patience bring results. 2:22-26.
  Against selfish pretenders in the church. 3:1-17.
    Avoid them. 3:5.
    They prey on those of restless minds who are ever curious but never grasp the truth. 3:6-9.
    Timothy must continue steadfast, remembering what he has learned from the Scripture and from Paul. 3:10-17.
A final charge. 4:1-8.
  "Preach the word." 4:2.
  So live as to have joy at the end. 4:6-8.
Personal messages. 4:9-18.
Greetings. 4:19-21
Blessing. 4:22.

Some personal directions complete the letter. These are among the last words Paul is ever to write, and he devotes them to news about persons whom Timothy knows or should know about. But before the final period could be placed, two words must be written again—

the greeting-word, precious and peculiarly Christian, "grace"; and the Name, above every name, the Lord Jesus Christ.

XII. The Letters to Titus and to Philemon

"My true child" and "our beloved."—Titus 1:4; Philemon 1.

At first glace the letters to Titus and to Philemon have little in common except that both are short.* The former is a business letter, the latter personal. Yet each deals with a specific problem which demanded an immediate solution. In each Paul presents his suggestions persuasively, in Philemon even lightheartedly, but still with apostolic authority.

Of Titus little is known. Acts does not mention his name. From references in Paul's letters certain facts can be established. Titus, a Gentile convert to Christianity, had gone with Paul and Barnabas on a mission to the Jerusalem church from Antioch, possibly Titus' native city. (Gal. 2:1, 3.) In II Timothy 4:10 we learn that Titus was then engaged in evangelizing Dalmatia, an area to the edge of which, Illyricum, Paul had gone (Rom. 15:19), but in which he had not personally labored. The Dalmatians were considered the wildest sort of barbarians; they were not finally conquered by the Romans until A.D. 9. In venturing among this people Titus had accepted what was perhaps the most hazardous of all "foreign" missionary assignments. At the time the letter to Titus was written he was on the island of Crete. (1:5.) This passage is our clearest evidence that Paul was able to make some missionary visitations between his first and his final Roman imprisonments. The Cretans, Paul plainly states, were rough folk, so that Titus' labors here, too, involved personal qualities of courage and faith.

The most we know about Titus is by casual reference in the Corinthian crisis. The Corinthian church rebelled against Paul's authority because he had sharply rebuked their petty wranglings.

---

* The order of Paul's letters in our English Bibles appears to have been based roughly on length. Number of chapters: Romans, 16; I Corinthians, 16; II Corinthians, 13; Galatians, 6; Ephesians, 6; Philippians, 4; Colossians, 4; I Thessalonians, 5; II Thessalonians, 3; I Timothy, 6; II Timothy, 4; Titus, 3; Philemon, 1.

Paul's quick personal visit to Corinth from Ephesus was unsuccessful. Paul then wrote a "severe" letter. It took courage and diplomatic tact to deliver that kind of letter at such a time. But Titus was the man to do it. He not only delivered the letter but, one supposes, by his earnest and sincere concern for his fellow Gentile Christians at Corinth succeeded in reuniting a divided church, winning back its respect for Paul. Such a helper was Titus to Paul and such a man was Titus.

Titus' task on Crete was to win for Christ enough Cretans, whom "everyone" said were liars, brutes, lazy, gluttons, and unchaste, to form a church. He was to find godly men to be its officers—men who would be able to perpetuate the redemptive power of Christ in the midst of a dissolute population. Titus had accepted that work. Paul's letter is a guide for Titus' endeavors.

An Outline for the Study of Titus

Salutation. 1:1-4.
  A reminder of his high calling.
Church officers. 1:5-9.
  Their qualifications.
The Christian attitude to take toward Judaizers. 1:10-16.
  (See page 141 for a discussion of the Judaizers.)
  Cretans characterized. 1:12.
Salvation in Christ is for all classes of men. 2:1-15.
Christian attitudes. 3:1-11.
  Toward organized society. 3:1-8.
  Toward teachers of false doctrine. 3:9-11.
Personal directions and remembrances. 3:12-14.
Greeting and benediction. 3:15.

Titus 2:11-14 and 3:4-7 are two fine, compact statements of the gospel according to Paul; they will repay careful study.

The narrative background of the letter to Philemon is well known. The letter's significance lies in what is revealed in the character of Paul, his sensitivity to doing the right thing whatever the consequences and his graciousness and gentleness in dealing with friends.

Philemon, a wealthy resident of Colossae, was a convert of Paul's.

He may have been a product of Paul's preaching at Ephesus. Onesimus, one of Philemon's slaves, had escaped, perhaps with some of Philemon's money. Onesimus had been attracted to Rome. There he learned to know Paul, and through him to know Christ. It was this that posed the problem: should Onesimus as a Christian now return, running the risk of being crucified, for that was the legal punishment for runaway slaves? Could Onesimus be faithful to his new-found Lord in any other way? On the other hand, did Paul as a friend of Philemon, a fellow Christian, have any alternative but to send Onesimus back to his master, even though it might be sending the slave to the cross? It was a tangled problem, and the only apparent solutions involved serious risks.

It is unsatisfying not to know whether the ending of the story was happy or tragic. What we do know is Paul's proposed solution to the problem. The Apostle insisted that Onesimus return to his master whatever the consequences. Paul understood the pressure fellow slave owners would put on Philemon to make an example of Onesimus by harsh punishment. To provide every possible protection for the slave-convert, Paul did four things. First, he sent Onesimus back not alone but with Tychicus who carried Paul's letter to the Colossians and perhaps the letter to the Ephesians. Secondly, Paul wrote our letter to Philemon for Onesimus to take with him. Thirdly, Paul addressed this letter to "the church in thy house," which would make the whole matter a subject of public knowledge. Perhaps the encouragement of the church would help to offset some of the pressure exerted by other slave owners. And finally, if the phrase "the epistle from Laodicea" in Colossians 4:16 refers, as it may, to Philemon, Paul requested that the Philemon letter be read to the Christians at Colossae as well, adding so much more to the weight of Christian public opinion. The life of one of Paul's friends was in the balance and the Christian integrity of another was in the balance, and Paul was anxious that neither the life of one nor the soul of the other should perish.

The letter to Philemon Paul carefully wrote to state the facts, to make an appeal, and to offer a proposal.

An Outline for the Study of Philemon

Salutation. 1-3.
Thanksgiving. 4-5.
Prayer. 6-7.
The appeal. 8-16.
    Not a command. 8-9, 14.
    For Onesimus. 10-13. (Is there an implied request in vs. 13?)
    The runaway explained? 15.
The proposal. 17-20.
    "As myself." 17.
    Who will pay the possible damages? 18-19.
    The urgency. 20.
Confidence and greetings. 21-24.
The blessing. 25.

The whole incident must have given the original readers of the letter, as it has those who have read it since, a very real exercise of mind and heart to find the Christlike line of action in a situation where the well-being of a number of his followers was involved.

"The grace of our Lord Jesus Christ be with your spirit. Amen."

HEBREWS
AND GENERAL LETTER

HEBREWS through JUDE

HENRY WADE DUBOSE

HEBREWS AND GENERAL LETTERS

THE EPISTLE TO THE HEBREWS

    The More Excellent Name. 1:1—4:13.

    The More Excellent High Priest. 4:14—7:28.

    The More Excellent Sacrifice. 8:1—10:18.

    The More Excellent Faith. 10:19—13:25.

THE EPISTLE OF JAMES

THE FIRST EPISTLE OF PETER

THE SECOND EPISTLE OF PETER

THE FIRST EPISTLE OF JOHN

THE SECOND EPISTLE OF JOHN

THE THIRD EPISTLE OF JOHN

THE EPISTLE OF JUDE

HEBREWS
AND GENERAL LETTERS

THE EPISTLE TO THE HEBREWS

The Epistle to the Hebrews is a letter to Hebrew Christians who were in danger of becoming like the hearers whom Jesus compared to the stony ground in the parable of the soils. (See Matthew 13:1-17; Mark 4:1-20; Luke 8:4-15.) They had accepted the Christian faith with great joy but were in danger of giving up their newly found faith for the old Judaism. Having once tasted the spiritual power of God, they were now tempted to fall back into a materialistic conception of God's Kingdom as it was transmitted to them in the ritualistic system of their forefathers. They desired a living faith, but had found the discipline of the Christian race more severe than they had at first anticipated. Therefore a Christian leader—some say Paul, others Barnabas, still others Apollos, Clement of Rome, or Priscilla—wrote this Epistle to bolster the faith of these Christians, and to inspire them to move forward rather than backward in the Christian faith. (See Dummelow's commentary and the Westminster Bible dictionary on date, authorship, and aim of the letter.)

This Epistle may be divided for study into these four divisions: The More Excellent Name, 1:1—4:13; The More Excellent High Priest, 4:14—7:28; The More Excellent Sacrifice, 8:1—10:18; and The More Excellent Faith, 10:19—13:25. While these divisions do not constitute a perfect outline of the book, they approximate it and give a basis for a four-unit study of the letter. Let us consider these divisions in the order named.

THE MORE EXCELLENT NAME
Hebrews 1:1—4:13

The first section opens with a key statement, "God hath spoken," but this statement is embellished by many descriptive words and phrases. Although he spoke through the prophets in many degrees and in divers manners, he has spoken in the latter days in his Son, the heir, the agent in creation, the expression of his glory, the incarnation of his Person, the forgiver of sins, and the exaltation of his majesty. (1:1-3.) This Son is not only better than the prophets but also better than the angels, having inherited a more excellent name than they. This is proved by the title given him by the Father, by the worship accorded the Son by the angels, by the Son's work of creation, and by the Son's exalted station over the angels, who are but ministering spirits of God to those who shall inherit salvation. (1:4-14.) Therefore the writer interrupts his argument to exhort the readers to give more earnest heed to the message which came from God through the Son and his apostles, for this word is more sure than the word even of angels, having the verification of miracles and of the Holy Spirit. (2:1-4.) While this exalted Son took upon himself human flesh for the sake of redeeming mankind, his self-imposed limitations did not make him less than the angels, but rather greater; "for it became him, for whom are all things, and through whom are all things, in bringing many sons unto glory, to make the author of their salvation perfect through sufferings." He partook of all the limitations of the flesh in order that he might make believers like himself, bringing them into the very family of God. He thus became the perfect High Priest, for he who was God entered completely into the temptations of man in order that he might succor men who were tempted. (2:5-18.)

This High Priest made believers partakers of a holy calling, one much greater than that of Moses. For as Moses was a faithful servant in the house of Israel, so Jesus is the Son in the house of Christianity, bidding his own hold fast their hope unto the end. (3:1-6.) Christians ought to give more earnest heed to the exhortation of Scripture, "To-day if ye shall hear his voice, harden not your hearts." (Cf. Psalm 95:7ff.) For the children of Israel refused to enter into the land of promise because they hardened their hearts against God, provoking him to anger. Thus by their disobedience and unbelief they failed to enter into the promised rest of God. (3:7-19.) Therefore we who have a higher calling—that is, a spiritual inheritance rather than a physical—must exercise a greater faith if we are to experience the satisfaction and achievement promised unto us as Christians. This satisfaction is like that which God had when he saw the result of creation, that it was good, and therefore rested on the Sabbath day. It was this kind of rest of which the psalmist spoke when he urged his hearers to be responsive to the voice of God. (4:1-7.) Although some may say that the promises to Moses were fulfilled in Joshua's time, the entrance into Canaan was but a foretaste of what God had in store for his people; it was but a physical type of the spiritual Kingdom which God had in mind for the Christian church. It was not the real thing, but an understandable symbol of the reality yet to be. (4:8-10.) Therefore, because God has revealed himself in the Son as well as in the angels and the prophets, because his revelation in the Son is much more excellent than other revelations, and because it is terribly dangerous to reject God's word through lack of faith and disobedience, let us diligently seek to enter into the greater satisfaction of Christian experience, which is the real rest of God, lest we fall after the same example of disobedience. For God's word is alive. It is sharper than a two-edged sword. It gets to the very heart of soul and spirit, as a light which shines upon the very thoughts and intents of the heart. This word brings all men before the eternal God, turning the searchlight on them and laying them open to the searching gaze of the Omniscient. (4:11-13.) Thus the name of the Son is more excellent than that of prophets or angels, Moses or Joshua, because in his character he brings God directly to man at the same time that he brings man directly before God.

THE MORE EXCELLENT HIGH PRIEST

Hebrews 4:14—7:28

The first section showed how Christ had obtained a more excellent name than any other agents used in God's revelation of himself, by bringing a more excellent revelation from God—a more complete and accurate revelation, a more personal and active revelation, and a more sacrificial and redemptive revelation. The purpose was to stir Christians, including Hebrew Christians tempted to drift back into materialistic traditions, to move forward in their experience to a spiritual and transforming faith. The priestly religion of the Jews was characterized by a concern for ritual which did not reach down into the moral depths of life. Yet the prophetic and transforming religion of the early church went to the depths of human sin and reached the heights of human achievement. Why this difference? The church had Jesus Christ as its Saviour and its great High Priest. It found a way of worship superior to the worship of Judaism because its worship brought the power it needed for victory over sin and for adventure in faith. The Jews said, "We have a priest who understands our weakness and offers our sacrifices to God." This writer said, "We have a High Priest far more excellent than the priesthood of Aaron." Let us see how he developed this idea.

The argument is opened with a twofold exhortation in 4:14-16. Because we have the High Priest who is so exalted, let us hold fast our confession; because we have the High Priest who understands our infirmities so completely, let us draw near with boldness to the throne of grace to find help as we need it. The Jews had feared to approach God; only the high priest dared do that and he only once a year. But any man or woman could draw near to God's throne of grace now, for Christ had opened the way to God even as he had brought God so completely to man. The writer continues to show how Christ fulfills the requirements for priesthood. He is one of the people, having been man; he offers sacrifice for sin, especially for the sins of the people; he does not take the honor, but is called by God, not to merely an Aaronic priesthood, but to the priesthood of the order of Melchizedek. (5:1-6.) Furthermore, this priest has been morally perfect amid bitter temptations; he has been made perfect through sufferings that he might become the captain of salvation for believers, for all who obey him. (5:7-10.)

The author pauses a moment, realizing that his doctrine is too far advanced for some of his readers. He throws in an interlude which continues through chapter 6. Then he picks up the argument again in chapter 7. (Note how you may read from 5:10 on to 7:1 without a break.) What is this digression which breaks into the argument? Why does it come at this point? Because the readers have become dull of hearing. Instead of having become teachers, they need to be taught again the first principles of Christianity. They have not put the power of God in Christ to work in everyday life; they have tried to believe without experiencing the truth of the things believed. They have sought a lazy man's religion like the one they had in Judaism. They want to be spoon-fed on milk rather than to chew and digest meat; they would be babies rather than full-grown men. (5:11-14.)

The writer, understanding clearly that in the Christian life one must either go forward or slip backward, exhorted his readers to press on to perfection. The idea of the word is purposeful. So, says the writer, let us press on to the use which the great God intended our lives should have. We were meant to be lights in the darkness; doctors in the sickroom; comforters to the bereaved; messengers of peace to the warlike; a tonic to the discouraged; a challenge to the indifferent; a source of strength to the weak; a messenger of eternal salvation to the sin-sick. Why should we go back to the first principles of repentance from dead works and of faith unto God? Of baptism and the laying on of hands? Of the resurrection and eternal judgment? See how impossible it is to renew those who tasted of the power of the Spirit of God and then, like Judas, fell away! See how that sort of conduct crucifies Christ afresh, doing away with his effectual sacrifice on Calvary! That makes no more sense than it does for ground blessed by God and cultivated by man to bring forth thorns and thistles. It is unthinkable that we should turn back if we have really been genuine in our earlier experience! (6:1-8.)

Of course you will not do that. You have borne the fruit of the Spirit in your love and service, so we are confident that you will show all diligence and persistence and faith to inherit the full promises of God, even as those who have already inherited his promises have done. (6:9-12.) Take, for instance, God's covenant with Abraham to bless him and make him a blessing. Abraham held fast in faith to the promise of God and God honored his faith. But this was not the whole purpose of God. He wanted to give to the spiritual seed of Abraham, to those who would exercise a like faith in a greater revelation of God, something much greater. Because of the unchangeable purpose of God, which is an anchor to our soul, we make bold to pierce the veil of God's redemptive purpose through Christ the forerunner, who is our High Priest after the order of Melchizedek. (6:13-20.)

Now let us consider Christ as the more excellent High Priest. When Melchizedek entered the story of Genesis 14 as a high priest to whom Abraham offered a tenth part of his spoils, he entered as a man whose genealogy was omitted, whose death was not recorded, and whose moral character as king of righteousness and king of peace was recognized. (7:1-3.) Think of the greatness of this priest as recognized in Abraham's offering of tithes to him. The Levites take tithes of the seed of Abraham according to Jewish law; yet here is a man greater than the father of the seed of Abraham. Therefore Melchizedek is greater than Abraham. (7:4-10.) Consider further that if the Levitical priesthood were perfect and complete, there would never have been a need for any other order of priests. Yet actually God raised up Jesus, who was of the tribe of Judah, to be a priest after the order of Melchizedek. (7:11-17.) By this God not only established a new order of priesthood, but he also disannulled the old law which established the Aaronic order of priests. Why? Because what the former order failed to accomplish, Jesus Christ did accomplish. So Jesus Christ is not a priest of an earthly or physical order, as of birth in a priestly line. His priesthood is unchangeable, for he abideth forever. "Wherefore also he is able to save to the uttermost them that draw near unto God through him, seeing he ever liveth to make intercession for them." (7:18-25.) In addition, this High Priest, perfect and blameless in character, willingly offered up himself *once for all* and has no need to enter daily into the sanctuary of God. His priestly sacrifice was not of bulls and goats, but of himself who had been made perfect through sufferings and who was eternally exalted in the heavens to make intercession for all who come to God through him. (7:26-28.)

How now can you Hebrews say that you want a high priest and an order of Aaronic priests? Why ask for the lower order when you may have the higher? Why ask for a stone when you may have bread? Or for a serpent when you may have a fish? Your old priestly order with all its failures and imperfections is done away. We have him who is above all and through all and in all, our Saviour, our Friend, God's eternal Son, our High Priest and Intercessor. Let us move forward to honor him with heroic living!

THE MORE EXCELLENT SACRIFICE

Hebrews 8:1—10:18

Each of the sections of this letter leads up to the next. The section which begins with chapter 8 looks both backward and forward, for it deals with the most basic problem of the book. "The chief point I am seeking to emphasize," the writer said to the Hebrews steeped in a priestly religion, "is that Christ is our exalted High Priest in a better worship than that which you gave up." If they could learn his importance and his function in worship they could experience his power to live in active faith; if they missed his function in giving power through their worship, they must needs slip back into a legalistic and ritualistic Judaism. The purpose is not just to emphasize Christ as a Person, but to show how Christ is the more excellent Sacrifice and the Mediator of a more excellent covenant.

The argument proceeds as follows: First, Christ is not a minister of the earthly tabernacle which man pitched, but of the heavenly tabernacle which God pitched. The earthly tabernacle outlined for Moses in the mount was but an imitation and an earthly copy of the eternal tabernacle of God in heaven. (8:1-5.) Furthermore, the High Priest in heaven is the mediator of a more excellent covenant than that which was associated with the earthly tabernacle, even the new covenant of God with the human heart announced by Jeremiah. (Jer. 31:31-34.) As God dwelt in human hearts they would know him directly and would find the old covenant supplanted by the new and living covenant mediated by Christ. (8:6-13.) This covenant is therefore far superior to the old covenant of which the tabernacle was but a symbol, for it brings God into the human heart and brings the human heart into the presence of the living God.

Yet you ask, How can Christ give to us what we received on the Day of Atonement, when we brought our sins to the tabernacle to receive through our sacrifice some sense of forgiveness? Let us consider this question for a few moments. You had in the earthly tabernacle several symbols: the candlestick, the table, the shewbread in the Holy Place, and then behind the altar of incense and the veil which separated the Holy Place from the Holy of Holies, you had the ark of the covenant with its contents. In the Holy Place the priests offered sacrifices at various times, but on the great Day of the Atonement the high priest entered the Holy of Holies once a year to offer a prayer for himself and for the sins of the people. (Lev. 16.) While all of this brought some satisfaction, it kept alive the fact that God himself was inaccessible to the common man, yea, even to the high priest himself. Therefore this whole sacrificial system, while good in its way, did not meet the full need of man for forgiveness or for access into the presence of the living God. (9:1-10.)

However, when we consider the ministry of Christ in the heavenly tabernacle, we find all this changed. He did not have to enter once a year to offer the blood of goats and calves, which was but a symbol of the life of sinners offered in sacrifice; he rather entered *once for all* into the Holy Place, offering his own blood—that is, his life—to obtain eternal redemption for believers. He himself is the perfect Sacrifice, the Mediator of the better covenant between God and the human heart. (9:11-12.) For if the blood of bulls and goats had any efficacy, and by faith it did for your forefathers, then "how much more shall the blood of Christ, who through his eternal Spirit offered himself without blemish unto God, cleanse your conscience from dead works to serve the living God?" The answer must be in the affirmative and constitutes the crux of the matter. His purpose was to make all the promises of the old covenant more sure in the new, not once a year but for all time. Where the ministry of the old covenant cleansed the vessels and the flesh, this ministry cleanses the human heart. (9:13-22.)

Again let me emphasize, the earthly ministry of the Aaronic priesthood was but an imitation of the ministry of Christ in the heavenly tabernacle. It required an annual atonement, while Christ voluntarily offered himself once for all for man's sin, making himself not only a Judge, but also a Saviour. (9:23-28.) If it had been possible for the law and the sacrifice of the old covenant really to cleanse worshipers, they would not have required an annual ceremony. Sacrifice is required for remission, to be sure, but only the perfect obedience and the perfect sacrifice of Christ can have the "once for all" character which the eternal God requires. This sacrifice supplants not only the "once a year" atonement, but also the daily sacrifices which in their smaller way have the same purpose. Thus with one offering of himself Christ becomes the perfect Sacrifice for sin for all time. This is the Sacrifice which is more excellent than the old sacrifices and which mediates the new covenant, better than the old. It mediates the covenant of God in the heart looked for by Jeremiah under the guidance of God's Spirit. (10:1-18.)

Because of this more excellent Sacrifice we are prepared to stop looking to the past and to keep on looking to the future; to cease asking for symbols and shadows when we may lay hold in faith on the reality; to leave behind the worship of God by proxy and to worship him in spirit and in truth.

The More Excellent Faith

Hebrews 10:19—13:25

The turning point of the letter to the Hebrews comes at 10:19, for all that goes before is preliminary to this threefold interpretation of the meaning of Christ's sacrifice for the church. This central redemptive act of Christ means, first, that he opened to all believers a new and living way to God and a new and living way to heroic endeavor. Therefore it means, secondly, that instead of being afraid to draw near to God we have an urgent and standing invitation to enter into his presence with all boldness. It means, thirdly, that we are given power to hold fast our confession and to encourage each other in love and good works. (10:19-25.)

Let us examine these three meanings more in detail. Consider the alternative to that confidence by which we draw near in faith to the living God. What is it but judgment and death, as a man under the law was judged by the mouth of two or three witnesses? How much greater punishment shall come to those who trample under foot the great redemptive sacrifice of Jesus Christ! It is a fearful thing to fall into the hands of the living God. (10:26-31.)

By way of contrast, recall the deep and abiding joy you experienced when you were made a laughing-stock, when you partook of the afflictions of your brethren, when you willingly gave up your earthly possessions because your heavenly possessions were so real. You have need of greater steadfastness under affliction that you may realize that, "having done the will of God, ye may receive the promise." For really we know that the righteous must live in his faith and faithfulness. For we are not the sort that shrink back into perdition, but rather those who march forward in faith to the winning of our souls. (10:32-39.)

Be fully assured that such a saving faith is full confidence in things believed in and hoped for, that it is the experienced evidence or conviction of heavenly realities such as those of which I have been writing; that is, of things not seen with the physical eye. This faith is the key to the whole of life from beginning to end, from the beginning of history to its consummation. Faith gives understanding of the way in which God made the universe. It is the means by which all the saints lived adventurously and themselves received the promises of God. Consider Abel, who offered a more excellent sacrifice than Cain; or Enoch, who was translated because he was well-pleasing to God; or Noah, who became heir of the righteousness which follows faith; or Abraham, who obeyed and found God more than faithful to his promises, as did also Isaac, Jacob, and Sarah. (11:1-12.) All of these even went to their death in faith, having been pilgrims and strangers on the earth, feeling a dim and strange longing after something better than an earthly inheritance, namely a heavenly inheritance. (11:13-16.) For this reason Abraham dared to offer Isaac as a sacrifice, being confident that, if necessary, God could raise him from the dead; Isaac also blessed Jacob and Esau; Jacob, worshiping, blessed the sons of Joseph; Joseph, seeing that his end was near, yet being confident that God would take his people back to Canaan, commanded that his bones be preserved and eventually buried in Canaan; Moses, having been protected at birth, chose in maturity to lead God's people rather than enjoy the pleasures of the sinful court of Egypt for a season, looking forward by example to the sacrifice of Christ; he led God's people out, establishing the Passover as a sign of God's covenant with his people. By this same faith Jericho was conquered and Rahab was saved. (11:17-31.) Time does not permit the completion of the roll call of the heroes and heroines of the faith, who subdued kingdoms and wrought righteousness, who obtained the promises of God through the fiery trials of suffering. Women received their dead, as it were, a symbol to them of a better inheritance beyond this life. No kind of persecution could make these heroes and heroines falter in their faith, for they looked for the greater promises of God which are now being fulfilled in us. (11:32-40.)

Therefore with this cloud of witnesses, let us give up every hindrance and every sin which so easily besets us, and let us run with steadfastness the race which is given to us, keeping our eyes on Jesus the initiator and the completer of our faith. For he is pre-eminently the Hero of faith. Keeping his eyes on the fruit of his sacrifice, he was willing to despise the shame and suffering of the cross. Even so we must not falter or fail when oppressed by enemies. (12:1-4.)

Some of you do not understand your present suffering, thinking that God has forsaken you. That is not the case. He is nearer to you in suffering than at any other time, for he is making you into the sons you are called to be. Although your chastening seems grievous, it has a redemptive purpose and leads to greater righteousness. (12:5-11.) Therefore help one another in your weakness, following after peace and striving for the completion of God's purpose in your lives. To this end tolerate no defilement of the body, neither accept a fleshly reward instead of a heavenly, as Esau did when he sold his birthright. (12:12-17.)

When God appeared to Moses on Mount Sinai he established a covenant at a time when the people feared to come into his presence. However, when Christ came he established a new Kingdom, a heavenly Kingdom which is as far superior to the earthly Jerusalem as the earthly Jerusalem, Mount Zion, is to Mount Sinai. Therefore, we must not fall short of the heavenly Kingdom any more than they were to fall short of God's will on Mount Sinai. (12:18-29.)

Be diligent also to apply your faith in everyday life: in love to the brethren, in hospitality, in sympathy for those who suffer, in honor in the marriage relationship, in putting love to God above love for money and being content with what you have. Secure in the promises of God we need fear nothing. (13:1-6.) Remember your leaders, who taught you the word of God, and consider the result of their manner of life. Jesus Christ is the same today as then. Let us beware of false teachers who would take away our inheritance in him, and let us dare to suffer reproach as Jesus did rather than to give up our faith in that heavenly Kingdom prepared for us. (13:7-14.) Let us also make our sacrifice to God a sacrifice of praise, of testimony, of good works, of obedience and submission to our real, spiritual teachers. (13:15-19.) To this end you must have the power of God in Christ. Bear this word of exhortation, for I hope shortly to come with Timothy, recently released from prison, to visit you. Your friends in Italy send greetings. (13:20-25.)

A final word should be said concerning the appropriateness of the benediction (vss. 20-21) with which this letter closes. It is a prayer that the God of peace who raised Jesus Christ from the dead through an eternal covenant may make our lives perfect, in every good thing to accomplish his will, working in us that which is well pleasing in his sight, "through Jesus Christ; to whom be the glory for ever and ever. Amen." Thus to the last the message of undying hope is maintained.

THE EPISTLE OF JAMES

Its Purpose

This is a very practical book. It was written not to elaborate Christian doctrine but to teach Christians how to live. It throbs with a passion for righteousness and pleads for reality and consistency in the Christian life. Keenly aware of the power of temptation and the weakness of human nature, the author exhorts professed followers of Christ to seek wisdom from God and to guard against deceiving themselves. He argues that the only faith that is real is a faith that produces Christian character and issues in good deeds. A religion that does not produce good in men does not save their souls.

Author

The author of this Epistle introduces himself as "James, a servant of God and of the Lord Jesus Christ." He was not James the brother of the Apostle John. That apostle was beheaded by Herod early in the Christian era. (Acts 12:2.) There was another apostle called "James the Less," of whom we know nothing except that he was one of the twelve. But we know also that Jesus had a brother named James. (Matt. 13:55.) And we know that during the momentous days between the Lord's resurrection and Pentecost, Mary the mother of Jesus and his brethren were among the disciples in Jerusalem. There James "the Lord's brother" later attained a position of authority comparable to that of the leading apostles. (Gal. 1:19 and Acts 15:13.) He became the leader of the church in Jerusalem, which was composed of Jewish Christians. He became, we believe, the author of this Epistle. (For a fuller statement of reasons for this belief see Dummelow's commentary.)

Readers

Addressed to "the twelve tribes which were scattered abroad," the letter was primarily a message to Jewish Christians, who were passing through great trials. In it the influence of the Old Testament is strong. It throbs with the spirit of the prophets. Exalting Jesus Christ as the Lord of Glory, James stresses his ethical teachings as the test and fruit of true faith. The author ardently exhorts his readers to live as professed believers ought to live. "Be ye doers of the word, and not hearers only." (Note James 1:3-4, 22; 2:18; 4:7-8; and 5:19-20.)

Analysis of the Book

In the first chapter James speaks of the "manifold temptations" which beset the followers of Christ, and how to triumph over them. Temptation means trial or testing. The Christian is tested both by outward circumstances (1:9-11), and by his own sinful desires (1:12-15).

To meet the tests successfully he must seek wisdom from God (1:5-8) and subject his natural impulses to the authority of the Word of God (1:17-25). As tests of the reality of one's religion James proposes control of the tongue, kindness to those who are unfortunate, and cleanness of life. (1:26-27.)

In the second chapter the author contends that true religion is tested by the way we treat people.

The natural man is prone to judge people by appearances, to respect those whose outward circumstances seem to mark them as superior, to despise those whom he regards as inferiors. This leads to unfair discrimination, to favoring adulation toward the socially acceptable, to snobbish disdain toward the socially excluded. Nothing could be more inconsistent with the truly Christian spirit. As Robert Burns put it, "The rank is but the guinea stamp, The man's the gowd for a' that!" God looketh on the heart. The truly noble are those who trust and love him. James sharply denounces the partiality that puts a premium on the accidents of circumstance. (2:1-13.) It is both unreasonable and sinful. It repudiates the royal law of love. That law is all embracing. It is such teaching as this that makes Christianity a power for social reform wherever it is sincerely accepted. While James was expounding the gospel, he was sowing the seed of democracy.

In the second half of this chapter the author contends that Christian faith is tested by its effect upon human relations. (2:14-26.) In this famous passage the author is not contrasting faith and works. He enters no debate as to whether men are saved by faith or works. He is teaching that saving faith and good works are inseparable, related as the roots and fruit of a tree are related. The contrast is between a pretended faith that ends in profession, and the true faith that issues in Christian conduct. Dead orthodoxy is worthless. Real faith involves the heart and will as well as the mind. It commits men to a life of love which proves itself by loving deeds. Such was the faith of both the virtuous Abraham, and the redeemed harlot Rahab. (2:21-25.)

Having argued that the reality of a man's religion is tested by the way he meets trials, and by the way he treats people, James affirms in chapter 3 that one of the most searching tests is the way one uses his tongue.

To those who are his, God has promised wisdom. (1:5.) Wisdom or the want of it is displayed in how we talk. An unbridled tongue reveals an ungodly spirit. (1:26.) To this aspect of the Christian life James now returns with amazing vigor. First he warns his readers against rashly assuming the role of teacher. (3:1.) Then with vivid and picturesque language he dwells upon the perils that lurk in the tongue.

The tongue is a tiny member, but more difficult to control than a plunging ship or fiery steed. And what havoc it can cause! As fire carelessly handled may set a forest ablaze, careless words may fill the world with the fires of hell. With such figures of speech the inspired writer warns Christians to watch their speech, and be forever on guard against the shameful and disastrous evils into which an undisciplined tongue may betray them.

The chapter ends with a contrast between the spurious worldly wisdom that begets bitterness and strife, and the wisdom from above that is "first pure, then peaceable, gentle, easy to be entreated." What could be more incongruous than Christians discussing affairs of the Kingdom of Christ in a rancorous spirit, or with stubborn pride of opinion?

The purpose of this chapter, as of the whole Epistle, is intensely practical. It challenges professing Christians to consider their habits of speech, with a broad intimation that such a consideration, honestly engaged in, would send some of us to our knees with bitter shame and penitent confession.

Is the human race forever doomed to periodically destroy its young manhood in the hell of war? As he begins the fourth chapter of his Epistle, James digs down to the root of this question. "Whence come wars?" he asks. (4:1.) If we are ever to deal with the curse of war, and with the lesser forms of strife and cruelty that blight the lives of men, we must get at the cause of these evils, and seek an adequate cure. That is the conviction that guides the thought of James in this passage.

The cause of the feuds that embitter human relations he finds in the selfish and sensual desires of the human heart. (4:2-3.) The persistence of these desires betrays a worldly spirit and convicts their possessor of disloyalty to God. To be in love with the world and its pleasures is to be untrue to God, and to leave the half-committed disciple with a divided heart. (4:4-5.) Release from this miserable condition is to be found only through humble penitence. (4:6-10.) A right relation with God excludes not only the violent antagonisms that issue in open strife, but also harsh criticism and a censorious spirit. (4:11-12.) Here is a test of true religion that probes deep into the life of many who bear the name of Christ. "Judge not, that ye be not judged," said our Lord. God is the judge of the lives and motives of men. We are neither wise enough nor good enough to sit in judgment on our neighbors. In yielding to the temptation to do so, we are guilty of presumption and a want of that humility which is of the essence of a truly Christian spirit.

Christian humility not only cancels the spirit of criticism, but also prevents an arrogant self-confidence and disposes us to subject all our earthly plans to the will of God and trustfully accept the dispositions of his providence. (4:13-17.) To cultivate this attitude is both a proper expression of faith and a safeguard against bitter disappointments and heartbreaking discouragement.

Into the closing chapter of the Epistle, James packs prophet-like denunciation of social injustice, a tender plea for patience in suffering, a warning against profanity, and a comforting assurance that God answers prayer. Here are the passion for righteousness and the earnest insistence upon humble faith in God that have characterized the whole letter. Almost fiercely the author arraigns those who use their wealth and power to deprive the less fortunate of the just reward of their toil. (5:1-6.) The solemn warning to the selfish rich, who live in luxury while others are in want, indicts conditions not less actual today than when James wrote. The plea for patience in tribulation was never more timely than now. (5:7-11.) The protest against profanity challenges a generation strangely devoid of reverence. (5:12.) In the final passages James encourages his readers with the assurance that men of faith never pray in vain. At the same time he emphasizes the bonds of sympathy that should bind Christians together and constrain them to pray for one another. Whether a brother be ill in body or soul, it is a matter of vital concern to his fellow Christians. (5:13-18.) The crowning privilege of a Christian's life is to convert a sinner from his error and save a soul from death. (5:19-20.)

THE FIRST EPISTLE OF PETER

The Author

Simon Peter, the impulsive and often unstable disciple of the Gospels, and the courageous preacher and leader of the church in the book of Acts, has now become an inspired writer, and a great teacher of the deepest spiritual truths. The confidence of the Lord, whom he once denied and often grieved, has been fully justified.

Readers

The great Apostle is writing to Christians scattered throughout the provinces of Asia Minor. His primary aim is to fortify them against persecutions present and future. Many of these Christians were of Jewish blood. They were the objects of bitter hatred and constant hostility on the part of the Jews who rejected Christ. They suffered much in mind and estate. The violent persecutions promoted by the Roman government were yet to come. Doubtless the Apostle clearly foresaw them. Led of God to strengthen his fellow believers to meet these trials both present and impending, Peter wrote this letter, which has been a source of strength and encouragement to suffering Christians of all generations.

Its Purpose

The key word of the Epistle is hope. Its aim is twofold: first, to enable God's children to triumph over present distresses by seeing the blessings that lie beyond them; second, to inspire suffering disciples to live godly lives in spite of their trials. Someone has noted that suffering is mentioned sixteen times in the letter. We are reminded also to note the things that the Apostle calls precious. (1:7; 1:19; 2:4-6; 3:4.) "Christ the Strength of His People," "The Sufficiency of

Grace," and "Hope the Sustaining Gift of God" are phrases that have been employed to sum up the message of I Peter.

Analysis of the Book

An Introduction

In the opening verses, the Apostle salutes the Christians of Asia Minor to whom the Epistle was primarily addressed, reminding them of the grace of the Father, the Son, and the Holy Spirit, to whom they owe their salvation. This greeting is followed by a rapturous paean of praise to God for that eternal salvation in which the saints now rejoice in spite of trials, looking unto Jesus with faith and love and joy unspeakable, and awaiting the fuller realization of their blessed inheritance in heaven. (1:3-9.) This precious salvation was revealed in advance to the prophets and is an object of wonder to the angels. (1:10-12.)

Following this exalted introduction the Apostle devotes the remainder of the letter to counseling the Christians with respect to three great matters—their privileges, their duties, and their trials. Through all these runs an appeal for holiness. Sinners redeemed are called to be the holy children of the holy God.

The Privileges of the Redeemed

Exultantly recounted in the passage that extends from 1:13 through 2:10 are the privileges reserved for God's redeemed. These are made the basis of an appeal for holy living, fervent brotherly love, and spiritual growth. Reminded of their redemption by the precious blood of Christ and their second birth, the saints are exhorted to nourish their souls with the sincere milk of the Word of God. The distinctive character and spiritual mission of the people of God are vividly set forth in a figurative passage (2:4-9) in which Christians are seen as living stones built into God's temple, then as a holy priesthood to offer spiritual sacrifices acceptable to God. Called out of darkness into his marvelous light, Christians are to make known to men the glory and grace of God.

The Duties of Christians

The second major passage of the Epistle (2:11—4:11) emphasizes the duties of Christians in the various relations of life. Reminding us that we are strangers and pilgrims in the earth, that is, citizens of the heavenly kingdom, the Apostle warns us against the human desires that war against the spiritual life. The disciples were objects of persistent slander. They are called to disprove these accusations by such lives as would ultimately lead their accusers to glorify God. (2:11-12.)

As citizens, Christians are to be examples of loyalty and obedience to civil government, combining respect for human rights with reverence for God and love for the brotherhood. (2:13-17.)

As servants, God's children are to be faithful and patient even when unjustly treated, even as Christ was patient in suffering, when he bore our sins on the cross. (2:18-25.)

As wives and husbands, Christians must exemplify the spirit of Christ in their conduct toward each other. Wives are to be dutifully subject to their husbands, mindful of winning them to God by their behavior, preferring the beauty of a meek and quiet spirit to outward adornment. Husbands in turn are to honor their wives as fellow heirs with themselves of the grace of God. Husbands and wives in right relation with God will be faithful and helpful to each other. (3:1-7.)

Once again, all Christians are urged to be tenderhearted, loving and humble, even when mistreated. The appeal is emphasized by a quotation from the Thirty-fourth Psalm. Goodness tends to disarm hostility. But even under abuse the Christian must be patient and forbearing, like the Saviour who suffered for us even unto death, that he might bring us unto God. His suffering was not in vain. Through it he passed to his throne in glory, having "preached unto the spirits in prison"—an expression of which the commentators offer a variety of interpretations. In 3:21 the Apostle reminds us that baptism is but a symbol of Christ's cleansing us of sin. (3:8-22.)

Pointing again to Christ as our example in suffering (4:1-6) the author declares that suffering may serve to purify the soul that resists sinful desires in order to live according to the will of God. This choice inevitably exposes the Christian to the criticisms of sinners, but God is the Judge to be pleased.

In all these relationships Christians are exhorted (4:7-11) to live in the light of the coming of Christ, "as good stewards of the manifold grace of God," loving one another fervently, glorifying God.

The Trials of Christians

In the third major section of the Epistle (4:12—5:11) the author bases his plea for a holy living upon a frank recognition of trials. These the Christian must expect. Accepted according to the will of God, trials will become a means of spiritual blessing and of exceeding joy.

In the closing chapter Peter addresses a special appeal to elders of the church, calling himself a fellow elder, and promising a crown of glory to faithful spiritual leaders.

Then comes a final appeal to those who are younger—and to all Christians—to be humble, to trust God without anxiety, to be watchful against the Devil and steadfast in faith. Beyond our brief sufferings are the sure rewards of God.

Salutations

In closing the letter the Apostle mentions Silvanus, whom we know as Silas, the former companion of Paul, to whom Peter apparently dictated and by whom he may have sent the Epistle. He sends the greetings of Mark, and also says, "She that is in Babylon ... saluteth you." By many Babylon is here assumed to be a symbolical name for Rome, and some maintain that Peter was writing from that city and thus conveys the greetings of the church at Rome. "Peace be unto you all that are in Christ."

THE SECOND EPISTLE OF PETER

Authorship

Scholars are not agreed as to whether or not this letter was written by the Apostle Peter, whose name is used in the salutation. However, there is internal evidence pointing to Peter as the author. (See Dummelow and the Westminster Bible dictionary for a discussion of these problems.) Whether or not the author can be positively determined, the church has found this letter packed with inspired scriptural truth. A similarity in 2:1—3:7 suggests the possibility of dependence upon Jude, but inasmuch as both writers dealt with the same type of heresies, such dependence cannot be too dogmatically asserted. (See commentary on Jude for brief description of the Judaic-Gnostic heresies. If available, the introduction to J. B. Lightfoot's commentary on Colossians gives an excellent description of these heresies.)

Theme and Exhortation

The readers were Christians who had obtained "a like precious faith" in Christ. The theme is stated in 1:10-11 and may be summarized in the exhortation, "Give the more diligence to make your calling and election sure."

The salutation is not separated in thought from the first part of the letter, for it leads into a recognition of the precious promises and of the divine destiny of the readers. Because they have escaped from the corruption of the world through lust, the Christians are urged to heap up a series of graces one upon another: adding to faith virtue, to virtue knowledge, to knowledge self-control, to self-control steadfastness, to steadfastness godliness, to godliness brotherly kindness, and to brotherly kindness love. (1:5-7.) Unless they strive by the grace of God to develop these virtues, these Christians may miss their calling and may stumble into sin rather than grow into their heritage in Christ.

Analysis of the Book

Chapter 1 continues with a consideration of the foundations of the Christian faith which the writer is zealous to keep before his readers, especially since he must soon put off his earthly tabernacle. His hope is that after his death they will not forget his testimony and the foundations of the Christian faith. The author reminds his readers that their faith is built upon the testimony of one who was an eyewitness of the glory and power of the living Christ, whom he had seen transfigured in the holy mount. This passage argues for the apostolic authorship of the Epistle, for Peter did see the transfiguration and did hear the voice of God giving approval to his beloved Son. Peter has made these words more sure in his own experience, looking ever unto the same experience among his readers, for whom he hopes that the day-star may arise in their hearts. He insists that the Christian testimony is a sure interpretation of the character and the meaning of Christ because it is given under the guidance of the Holy Spirit. Special interpretations such as the Judaic-Gnostics give concerning the Person and the work of Christ are cunningly devised fables, but the apostolic and scriptural interpretation of prophecy is trustworthy. (1:12-21.)

Doctrinal Problems

Having given the doctrinal basis of his argument in the first chapter, the writer proceeds to deal with his problem in chapters 2 and 3. He points out clearly the danger from the false teachers who brought in destructive heresies, denying the Master his rightful place in the thought and life of the church. These false teachers prey upon the social and mental temptations of the people to enslave them, to make merchandise of them. These false teachers must be judged even as God judged the people in Noah's time and preserved righteous Noah, or destroyed Sodom and Gomorrah for their wickedness but saved Lot from this destruction. (Note the similarity between this whole argument and that of Jude.) All who live according to the lusts of the flesh and deny the authority of God shall likewise be brought to judgment. (2:1-11.)

Descriptions of False Teachers

In 2:12-22 the writer gives a vivid description of these false teachers. They are creatures without reason, speaking loudly about things of which they are ignorant, reveling in deceit, their eyes full of lust, their hearts covetous, their influence degrading, and their motive selfish even as Balaam's was when he was called upon to speak for God to Balak. They are "springs without water, and mists driven by

a storm; for whom the blackness of darkness hath been reserved."
(2:17.) They are as huge windbags being puffed up with vain words,
but full of the lusts of the flesh; as men promising freedom but turning freedom to license and hence to bondage; they are as men entangled in a net of legality who were freed by Christ, but who have
chosen to entangle themselves again in the net. Thus their last state
is worse than the first. They have created a moral and spiritual bog
and then have been drawn into it up to their armpits. It is filled with
quagmire of corruption so that it destroys all who permit themselves
to be caught in its power. (2:18-22.)

The Return of Christ

Chapter 3 opens with a reference to the fact that this is the second
letter which the writer has written, both being designed to stir up the
readers to remembrance. We may assume that this reference is to I
Peter, but the general import of that letter is encouragement under
trial rather than danger from heresy. It may be that the letter referred
to has not been preserved and that we have no record of it. At any
rate, in this letter the author deals with another problem, that of the
imminent return of the Lord. Some were beginning to doubt
whether Christ would come or whether there would be a day of
judgment. They are called mockers who inquire when the day of
his coming is. They argue that just as has always been the case, men
will die a natural death as they have since the creation. Peter suggests
that the very creation of the earth, raising it from the waters, was a
step toward judgment by fire. (3:1-7.) He points out that with God a
day may be as a thousand years, and a thousand years as a day. God
has been long-suffering, but the Lord will come suddenly and unex-
pectedly, as a thief in the night. Then will come the total destruction
of the present order. Because of this Christians should live in godliness and expectation, looking for the day of judgment and for a new
order. There are those who fail to apply these words to the first century and apply them only to the twentieth, but it is clear that an early
return of Christ was expected in the first century, and was a challenge to high and holy living. Although we know not when this
return is to be, we, too, ought to be living in all reverence and ex-

pectation, striving to create the Kingdom of God upon the earth. (3:8-13.)

Reference to Letters of Paul

The closing paragraph of this letter contains particular reference to the letters of Paul. After urging again full diligence in making their calling sure through steadfastness, realizing the redemptive purpose of Christ in long-suffering, the author refers to his brother Paul. He also refers to Paul's letters which speak of these things. Doubtless Paul's letters had been read to the churches addressed in this letter. Some did not understand Paul and tried to make something difficult out of his messages concerning the Christian faith. Here, however, the author is urging the Christians not to be misled by false interpreters, but to remain steadfast in the truth of the gospel, and thereby to grow in the grace and knowledge of his Saviour and theirs, even Jesus Christ.

This Epistle is a ringing challenge to *steadfastness in the Christian faith* in the face of false teachers who seek to mislead the faithful. It is also a plea for spiritual growth. It is a heroic effort to hold Christians true to their high calling in Christ Jesus.

THE FIRST EPISTLE OF JOHN

Authorship and Date

That the First Epistle of John was written by the author of the Gospel of John is apparent to the thoughtful reader, and the inference is confirmed by the testimony of the early church fathers. One has only to compare the first two verses of the Epistle with the prologue of the Gospel (John 1:1-18) to note the similarity in thought and style. Scholars find evidence of this identity of authorship all through the Epistle. (For an interesting presentation of this matter see the article on the Epistle in the Westminster Bible dictionary, p. 320.) For the belief that the author was the beloved Apostle John, evidence is supplied both by the early fathers and within the books themselves, although neither names its author. The two books were probably written about A.D. 90, and were certainly in circulation and highly esteemed by the church in the second century.

Purpose

There is a striking parallel between the two statements in which the author sets forth his purpose in writing these books. In the Gospel the Apostle says, "These are written, that ye might believe that Jesus is the Christ, the Son of God; and that believing ye may have life in his name." (John 20:31.) In the Epistle he says, "These things have I written unto you, that ye may know that ye have eternal life, even unto you that believe on the name of the Son of God." (I John 5:13.) The Gospel was written that men might believe, the Epistle to men who did believe. The theme of the Gospel is the deity of Christ. The theme of the Epistle is assurance of salvation. The aim of both was to establish believers in eternal life through Jesus Christ.

What does it mean to be a Christian? How is the Christian life distinguished from the natural life of men? This question John answers in two ways; first by defining the underlying experiences of the Christian life, then by stressing the outward evidences of this life. In its underlying experience, or inner nature, the Christian life is a life of fellowship with God, and it is that because those who have it have been born of the Spirit of God. When John speaks of the children of God he is not thinking of human beings in general, but of those who have been born again and are living in fellowship with God. The outward evidences of this spiritual life upon which the Apostle dwells are three: belief in Jesus Christ, obedience to the will of God, and love for God and men.

Analysis of the Book

The Epistle is simple in style, direct in teaching, tender in spirit, and rich in comfort. It is the counsel of a spiritual father to his "little children." The author speaks out of intimate acquaintance with Christ and out of a ripe assurance of eternal life. (1:1-2.)

His initial theme is fellowship. (1:3-7.) This happy fellowship with the Father, the Son, and other believers can only be obtained by walking in the light of God's will. The hindrance is sin, a blight that we cannot truthfully deny, but from which through sincere confession we can find a blessed deliverance. (1:8-10.)

In the second chapter, addressing believers as his little children, the Apostle speaks of the Lord Jesus Christ as our advocate, and as the propitiation for our sins. (2:1-2.) But how can we know that we know him? How can we know that we are his? There are sure proofs. (2:3-14.) One is obedience to the commandments of God. Another is love for the brethren. He appeals to different groups in the church—to little children, to fathers, to young men—to fully realize their salvation.

From the inner circle within which God's children enjoy a blessed fellowship, the Apostle glances at a hostile world that challenges their faith and opposes to its godliness an unholy way of life. (2:15-29.)

The Christian community must live in a world polluted by sensual desires ("the lust of the flesh"), a selfish covetousness ("the lust of the eyes"), and egotistical arrogance ("the vainglory of life"). It is all a vain show that will pass away. But Christians must be on their guard against its enticements. The love of the things that the world holds dear is quite incompatible with the love of God. (2:15-17.)

There are other dangers. Heresies have arisen. (2:18-27.) There are men who would pervert the gospel, some denying that Christ is divine, some denying his true humanity, some claiming to be Christians while they live willfully in sin. (See the Westminster Bible dictionary and Dummelow's commentary.)

Against these antichrists John lovingly warns his spiritual children, appealing for close fellowship with the Saviour and a life of consistent righteousness. False Christians fall away (2:19), but true believers know the truth and know that the proof of eternal life is righteousness. (2:28-29.) In all this, belief in Christ stands out as a proof of the spiritual life.

In the third chapter, the Apostle stresses righteousness (3:1-10) and love (3:11-24) as tests of the Christian life. He first rejoices in the high estate and blessed hope of those whom a loving God has called his sons. (3:1-3.) He reminds those who hope in Christ that they must purify themselves as Christ is pure.

The Christian cannot compromise with sin. (3:4-10.) There are verses in this chapter that seem to teach the sinless perfection of Christians even in this present world. But we know that Christians do fall into sin. And in the first two and last chapters of this Epistle the Apostle recognizes this fact. He counsels believers to seek forgiveness with confession of their sins. The difficulty is probably to be resolved by remembering that John is opposing false disciples who condoned sin, holding that it inhered in the flesh but did not affect the spirit of believers. Against this heresy John was adamant. There must be no compromise with sin. It is foreign to the Christian life, and deadly to the soul that consents to it. The Christian is committed to a sinless life. To its attainment he is bound to strive unceasingly, impelled by the new life that he has received, which is the life of God within him. Perfection is not yet attained, but "if he shall be manifested, we shall be like him." A Christian is a person who by the grace of God is being changed into the likeness of Jesus Christ. (Compare II Cor. 3:18.)

As a result of the essential opposition between the Christian life and the life of the world, the child of God may expect to be hated. (3:12-13.) But the Christian life is a life of love. That we love the brethren is a proof that we have passed from death unto life. To drive home this truth and unfold the true meaning of love the Apostle draws a contrast between Cain the murderer and Christ the perfect embodiment of love. Here we are reminded of the true nature of love. It is essentially sacrificial, the willingness of giving oneself for others. It proves its genuineness not by words but by deeds of helpfulness.

In the fourth chapter, the Apostle holds fast to his insistence that belief in Christ, love for one another, and righteous living are the marks of those who know God. But as his thought moves through the familiar cycle it reveals new insights and yields new implications.

There is a Babel of conflicting religious teachings. (4:1-6.) How are we to know the truth? How can we tell what teacher to trust? Every teacher is to be tested by what he says of Jesus Christ. The Spirit of God bears witness to the incarnation of the Son of God. He who denies that truth cannot be speaking by the Holy Spirit. He is a false prophet. His words are acceptable to the world but not to the children of God.

Coming again to love as an evidence of the Christian life, the Apostle explains why this must be so. (4:7-21.) It is because God is love. He, therefore, who is born of God and shares the life of God will inevitably manifest a loving spirit. Love is of the very essence of the spiritual life. The life of love can be attained by men only as they abide in God who is the source of love. But no man can truly claim to love God if he does not love his brothers. "We love because he first loved us."

In the opening verses of the fifth chapter the Apostle affirms again that the children of God are those who believe that Jesus is the Christ, and who love God and his children. With these two proofs of the spiritual life he ties in the third—the keeping of God's commandments. These three are inseparable elements of the faith that overcomes the world. (5:1-5.)

What evidence have we to support our faith in Christ? We have a threefold witness. (5:6-12.) We have the witness of our Lord's earthly life—its holiness symbolized by water, its atoning sacrifice symbolized by the blood. (See Dummelow's commentary.) We have the witness of the Holy Spirit, as he unfolds the meaning of our Lord's life and death in the Scripture and in our response to it. We have the witness of Christ's experience, in the peace and assurance of a believing heart.

This brings the Apostle to the climax of his message. In the concluding passage he sounds the grand Amen of Christian assurance. (5:13-21.) Seven times he uses the word "know." We know that we have eternal life. We know that God hears us when we pray. We know that we are to be done with sin. We know that we belong to God. We know that Jesus Christ is the Son of God and that our life is in him.

THE SECOND EPISTLE OF JOHN

The Second Epistle of John is a personal letter apparently addressed to a church or a group of churches. It deals with some of the same matters discussed in the first letter of John and with the subject of hospitality to travelers who claim to be teachers of Christian truth. (For other possible views on the meaning of "elect lady," see Dummelow's commentary and the Westminster Bible dictionary.) It is composed of a salutation (vss. 1-3), the main body of the letter (vss. 4-11), and a conclusion (vss. 12-13). The letter is addressed by the elder, whom we take to be the Apostle John, to those whom he loved and who knew the truth. He quickly identifies himself with the readers and expresses the conviction that grace, mercy, and peace from God the Father and Jesus Christ the Son will continue with himself as with them.

After expressing his joy at the true manner of life demonstrated by certain of the members of the community to which his letter is addressed, John makes his characteristic appeal for mutual affection, "that we love one another." This love means more than affection, it means also loving obedience to the will of God and loyalty to Christ. He warns his readers against the many false prophets in the world who deny the real incarnation of Jesus Christ. He urges his friends to examine themselves thoroughly that they may lose nothing of their testimony and that they may abide in the true teaching about God and Christ. So great is his concern that he warns against receiving hospitably any person who lacks a true doctrine of Christ, lest Christians become partakers of the evil works of false teachers. John promises to pay an early visit to his friends so that he may speak with them face to face. He closes the Epistle with a salutation from a sister church.

This letter emphasizes a genuine walk with Christ and a loyal devotion to true doctrine concerning the Person of Christ.

THE THIRD EPISTLE OF JOHN

This third letter of John deals with three men: Gaius, to whom it is addressed and who is highly praised for his hospitality to evangelists (vss. 1-8); Diotrephes, who is roundly scolded for his pride, and who is sternly denounced (vss. 9-11); and Demetrius, who receives commendation from all men (vs. 12). It closes with a message similar to that of II John. The author seems to be the same, but the problems are slightly different. (See Dummelow's commentary and the Westminster Bible dictionary for details as to authorship, date, etc.)

While this one-page letter is addressed to Gaius (probably not the helper of Paul), it presumes a church group with which he is closely associated. John is overjoyed to hear of the walk of Gaius (or Caius) in the truth; that is, in the love and fellowship and righteousness of God in Christ Jesus. He expresses the hope that Gaius may continue to prosper and be in health as his soul prospers. John praises Gaius especially for his hospitality to traveling evangelists, who at this time went from one group to another, and who were usually entertained by some member of the local church. Under the conditions then prevailing, the entertainment of Christian teachers contributed greatly to the spread of the gospel. Gaius had taken upon himself this duty as a service to Christ and his church, thus giving encouragement to true teachers of the Christian faith.

John turns his attention to Diotrephes, who loved to have first place in the local congregation, even to stirring up a spirit of rebellion against John when his former letter was received. (We cannot be sure whether or not this letter was II John.) Diotrephes had even rejected the true teachers who came to the church, and had cast out those who were willing to receive them. Gaius may have been one of these who were cast out. John proposes this test for Diotrephes: "He that doeth good is of God: he that doeth evil hath not seen God." Diotrephes' evil works are not to be imitated.

By way of contrast the author introduces the name of Demetrius (not the silversmith of Ephesus mentioned in Acts 19), who is highly spoken of by all men, including the writer himself. John will visit the church shortly and set things once more in order. The friends with him send greetings to each of their friends in Gaius' community, thus concluding a brief but practical letter primarily concerned with Christian living.

The Epistle heartily commends hospitality to the messengers of God and roundly reproves the effort of any man who would put himself in place of Christ as the head of the local church.

THE EPISTLE OF JUDE

Authorship and Date

This letter was written by Jude, who appears to have been the brother of Jesus and not one of the Apostles. (See Matt. 13:55; Mark 6:3; Acts 1:14.) It was addressed to the called who were beloved of God the Father and guarded by Jesus Christ. The salutation includes a prayer for the mercy, peace, and love of God to be multiplied in their behalf. (For details concerning the date, authorship, etc., see Dummelow's commentary and the Westminster Bible dictionary.)

Theme

The theme of Jude is introduced in verses 3 and 4. An emergency has arisen in the Christian community or communities to which this letter was addressed, due apparently to the Judaic-Gnostic heresy combatted by Paul in his letter to the Colossians. The Judaic emphasis on legalism rather than on faith in Christ as the means of salvation, and the Gnostic doctrine concerning Christ as a being very different from the divine-human Saviour of the Gospels, were the two most disturbing heresies of the early church, and were disseminated by certain false teachers who zealously went about from church to church. Because these false teachers threatened to undermine the truth about Christ and salvation, and because they rejected the high ethical standards of Christianity, the readers were urged to contend for the faith once for all delivered to the saints.

Warning to False Teachers

The argument is one steeped in Old Testament and inter-Testament tradition. It solemnly recalls the destruction of certain of the Hebrews who came out of Egypt, the punishment of angels who were bound because of their disobedience, the judgment upon Sodom and Gomorrah, upon murderous Cain and greedy Balaam and the rebellious Korah. These strange teachers must suffer a like end, for they have gone after fornication and wild speculation. They are like false shepherds, "clouds without water, carried along by winds; autumn trees without fruit, twice dead, plucked up by the roots; wild waves of the sea, foaming out their own shame; wandering stars, for whom the blackness of darkness hath been reserved for ever." God will call forth an array of angels to visit these selfish sinners and desperate murderers of his people. (Vss. 5-16.)

Duties of Christians

Jude then turns the thought of his readers to a series of duties which devolve upon them. He first counsels them to remember that the apostles have predicted that these false teachers would appear as mockers, as those who walk after their own ungodly lusts. He urges the Christians to grow in the faith, to keep on praying in the Holy Spirit, to abide in the love of God, and to keep looking for the mercy of the Lord Jesus Christ. He also exhorts them to have mercy on the weaker brethren troubled with doubts and to snatch them, as it were, out of the fire. They are enjoined to spare no efforts to rescue if possible some others who are tainted with false doctrine.

Benediction

The letter closes with an appropriate, beautiful, and impressive benediction. It ascribes endless glory and power to him who is able to keep his own from falling, to present them before his presence without blemish with great joy, even to the only wise God who became Saviour in Jesus Christ. Thus the timeless message couched in phrases of warning for a particular time is brought to its conclusion with a promise of God's victorious power.

THE REVELATION

JAMES E. BEAR

THE REVELATION

THE REVELATION

INTRODUCTION

Revelation is not an easy book to understand! We therefore strongly recommend that as a foundation the student study the content of Revelation for himself, seeking to see what is said, and also to see what divisions he can find in it. This study should be made with the American Standard Version or the Revised Standard Version which divide the text into paragraphs and also give a translation based on a better Greek text than that of the King James Version.

Because of the brevity of this survey we can only sketch the line of interpretation which seems best to us with our present understanding. No two interpreters will agree on all points, but students of the book do have to choose between several widely differing schools of interpretation, the chief of which are: (1) The Preterists, who put the message of the whole book in the past; (2) The Futurists, who put it all at the end of the age; (3) The Continuous History group, who find in it a sketch of church history; and (4) The Symbolists, who find stated in the book great spiritual truths good in every age.

Along with an increasing number of scholars today, we feel that the message of the book was primarily for John's readers and the problems of their day, but that it also has a message for the church through the ages, so we make a combination of the first and the fourth views. It is rooted in John's day and it has a message for us today.[1]

We recommend the following books for those who wish a fuller discussion than we have space to give. These books, with varying emphases, favor the combination viewpoint given above. The Westminster Bible dictionary has an excellent but brief article on "Revelation." Dummelow's one-volume commentary will give suggestive introductory material and comments. Donald W. Richardson's *The*

---

[1] For a fuller introductory statement see pp. 53-58 of this book. On schools of interpretation see also the Westminster Bible dictionary, p. 515; Richardson, pp. 42-44; Love, pp. 46-48; Dummelow, pp. 1066-1067.

Revelation of Jesus Christ presents a simple but rich exposition of the book. Julian Price Love's discussion of Revelation in the Layman's Bible Commentary (volume 25) has recently become available and offers real help for individuals and groups. Hendriksen's *More Than Conquerors* gives a somewhat fuller discussion than the others, and presents in simple language biblical arguments for the positions taken on disputed points. A comprehensive study by Albertus Pieters, *The Lamb, the Woman, and the Dragon,* has been reprinted under the title, *Studies in the Revelation of St. John.* Dr. Pieters presents the scenes of the book in graphic terms and summarizes the various points of view, arguing for his own, which is very satisfactory. The student, especially if he be a teacher, should not depend upon one commentary.

The Content of the Revelation

The Introduction. 1:1-8.

  I. *The Call to Conflict.* 1:9—3:22. The Living Christ, by praise, warning, and exhortation, prepares his church for the coming period of suffering.

  A. The Vision of the Living Christ Who Commands. 1:9-20.

  B. His Letters to the Seven Churches of Asia. Chapters 2 and 3.

  II. *The Course of the Conflict.* Chapters 4—20. This age-long conflict between the forces of good and evil is under God's control, and will be brought to an end by him.

  A. In Heaven—God Is Seen as the Master of the Situation. Chapters 4—11.

  1. The Vision of the Throne, the Book, and the Lamb. Chapters 4 and 5.

  2. The Seven Seals—giving the means and necessity for judgment. 6:1—8:1.

  a. First four seals—the means of judgment—the conquering gospel, war, famine, and death. 6:1-8.

  b. Seals five and six—the conscience of man expects judgment —the demand for the vindication of the right, and men's fear of God's wrath. 6:9-17.

  c. Parenthetical scenes—the safety of God's people, and the church in glory. Chapter 7.

    d. The seventh seal—silence—the judgment is not yet! 8:1.

3. The Seven Trumpets—marking the outpouring of judgment on the wicked which should lead to repentance. 8:2—11:19.

    a. The first four trumpets—judgment primarily on nature. 8:7-12.

    b. Fifth and sixth trumpets—judgment primarily on men, through evil spirits and through war. 8:13—9:21.

    c. Parenthetical scenes—the little book—a preview of the safety and the conflict of God's people. 10:1—11:13.

    d. The seventh trumpet—the final victory proclaimed. 11:14-19.

B. On Earth—Satan and His Allies Persecute the Church and Are Overthrown. Chapters 12-20.

1. The Persecution of the Church by Satanic Forces. Chapters 12—14.

    a. Satan, the real cause of the conflict, defeated by Christ but allowed to persecute the saints for a short time. Chapter 12.

    b. Satan's allies in John's day, the two beasts symbolizing the political and religious sides of the persecuting Roman Empire. Chapter 13.

    c. Parenthetical scene—the safety of the saints. 14:1-5.

    d. The announcement of judgment and the visions of the Harvest-Judgment. 14:6-20.

2. The Final Overthrow of the Satanic Forces Pictured. Chapters 15—20.

    a. The seven "bowls" poured out on those having the mark of the Beast. Chapters 15 and 16.

        (1) Parenthetical scene—the saints in glory rejoice in the vindication of the righteousness of God. 15:1-4.

        (2) The seven bowls poured out on those having the mark of the Beast and on "Babylon" the seat of the Beast. 15:5—16:21.

    b. The greatness of "Babylon" (Rome) and her judgment pictured. 17:1—19:10.

        (1) Her identity. Chapter 17.

        (2) Her fall proclaimed, and the sorrow of the kings and merchants and seamen over her fall. 18:1-19.

        (3) Joy in heaven over her fall. 18:20—19:10.

    c. The overthrow of the two "beasts." 19:11-21.

d. The overthrow of Satan himself. 20:1-10.
(1) The initial victory of Christ referred to (12:1-10),
Satan is "bound" for a season. 20:1-3.
(2) The glorious life of God's "overcomers." 20:4-6.
(3) Satan's final effort and his overthrow. 20:7-10.
e. The final judgment of all men. 20:11-15.

III. *The Consummation of the Conflict.* 21:1—22:5.

A. The New Heavens and the New Earth. 21:1-8.
B. The New Jerusalem. 21:9—22:5.

The Conclusion. 22:6-21.

I. ITS THEME AND ANALYSIS

Its Theme. The book was written to Christians who had suffered and were facing a more severe persecution. Its theme may best be suggested by these leading ideas: God reigns; through the slain Lamb, God's Kingdom will be established; sure judgment will fall upon the enemies of God; the people of God are under his special protection and those who overcome will share the blessedness he has for his people. These truths suggest the message of the book for God's distressed people.

Its Structure. It is generally agreed that the book is a unity and that it has a planned structure, but there is no general agreement as to how it is to be subdivided. Many regard chapters 1:1-8 and 22:6-21 as the introduction and the conclusion of the book. In the body of the book, distinct breaks seem to come between chapters 3 and 4, 11 and 12, and 20 and 21, thus making four main sections: chapters 1:9—3:22, the vision of Christ and his letters to the churches; chapters 4—11, the vision of the Throne, the Lamb, and the Book and what follows its unsealing; chapters 12—20, the Radiant Woman, her enemies and their overthrow; and chapters 21:1—22:5, the New Jerusalem.

The statement in 1:19 is commonly taken as a key to the book. In that case, "the things which thou sawest" refers to the vision of Christ (1:9-20); "the things which are" to the state of the seven churches of Asia (chapters 2—3); and "the things which shall come to pass hereafter" to coming events which are sketched in chapters 4:1—22:5. In regard to this prophetic part, we see that chapters 4—20 deal with the conflict of God (and his people) with the forces of evil, and chapters 21:1—22:5 with the state of God's people after the conflict is over.

John's readers will be helped to face the conflict by Christ's letters to them, and they will look toward the blessed future state with hope, but their eager interest will be in the central portion, and they will have questions to ask as they face suffering, even as God's saints today. They will ask, Why do the forces of evil persecute us? The answer will be, God has given them this power. Again, Does not God rule? Will he not punish the wicked? The answer is, Yes, even now he is bringing judgment upon them, and he will finally destroy them. Again they will ask, Will God save his faithful ones? The answer is, Yes. He may not keep them from suffering and death, but he will bring all who overcome into his glory.

As we study chapters 4—20 we will see that the prophecy starts with the people and events of John's own day; with the Christians who suffered then, and with the Roman Empire which persecuted them. But repeatedly, through these chapters, we are brought down to the end of the age by a pronouncement or a vision; for example: 6:16-17; 8:1; 14:14-20; 16:17-21; and 20:9-15. Thus the book seems to fall into sections, each starting with the situation in John's day and ending with a glance at the final victory of God. The primary message is for the immediate crisis, but looming up in the future beyond this present judgment of evil the prophet's eye sees the final victory of God at the end of the age. It was not given to him to see or to sketch the centuries between, but his vision enables him to say with confidence that God reigns and will triumph. The promise of victory over the actual forces of evil in John's day, however, is not without a message for the later church, for we will find those ancient embodiments of evil typical or similar to others found in every period of history, and God who is the same yesterday, and today, and forever may be counted on to act as he acted then.

The book, then, is not continuous prophecy, but a series of sections going over the same period, i.e., from John's day to the end, but with different emphases. How many of these sections are there? Some find seven parallel sections. We agree, however, with those who see two major sections of the conflict, chapters 4—11 and 12—20, the latter being distinguished from the former by a clearer emphasis on the enemies to be overcome. Each of these major sections, however, has subsections, which, as we shall see, cover in part the same period, from John's day to the end.[2]

II. THE PRINCIPLES OF INTERPRETATION

A Book of Symbolic Pictures. We have spoken of the "prophetic" part of Revelation, but as we read it we quickly see that the form of statement is different from that in most of the Old Testament prophetic writings (e.g., in Jeremiah), and reminds us of the visions in Daniel and in parts of Ezekiel and Zechariah. The prophet receives the truth through a vision and presents it in the form of a picture. Revelation, along with other such writings, belongs to a distinct class of writings called "apocalypses," whose purpose is to "unveil" or "reveal that which is hidden."[3] Their distinct mark is that the truth is presented not in plain statements of fact but in pictures. Moreover, these pictures are not like photographs of real things, but are *symbolic* pictures like our newspaper cartoons.[4] They are often absurd or ridiculous to the mind, but suggestive to the imagination.[5] The truth is there for the spiritual eye. But we make a mistake and will reach wrong conclusions if we apply to the pictures of this book the method of interpretation we would use, say, for the prophecy of Amos.

A Book of Symbolic Numbers. Revelation is full of numbers, and

---

[2] For a fuller discussion of the structure and message of Revelation see the books suggested in the introduction. It will also be of interest to compare their differing analyses.

[3] On Apocalyptic writings see Dummelow, p. 1065; Richardson, p. 16; Love, pp. 37-50.

[4] For example, the eagle symbolizes the U. S., the donkey the Democratic party, etc.

[5] E.g., in 1944 some cartoons represented the deep divisions in the Democratic and Republican parties by two new animals, each half elephant and half donkey. Or note the description of Christ in Revelation 1:16. Who would wish to paint his picture with a sword sticking out of his mouth!

we with our Western, literalistic minds are prone to take them at their face value. Seven is seven, we say, ten is ten, etc. But for the Oriental the Bible numbers had a symbolic significance which we often miss.[6] They are used singly and in combinations to suggest ideas. A familiar example is Peter's question,[7] "Forgive *seven* times," and Jesus' reply, "Not 7 times but 70 x 7," which is 10 x 7 x 7. Here both ten and seven have symbolic significance. So with the numbers of Revelation. Seven is the number of completeness, the divine number. Ten is the number of human completeness. Twelve is the number of organized religion. Four is the number of the earth, etc. There are multiples and fractions. One thousand is 10 x 10 x 10; 144,000 is 12 x 12 x 1000; etc. Half of seven is common to the book—3½ years (with its equivalents, 42 months, 1260 days), and time, times, and a half a time. Therefore, as we study Revelation let us seek the meaning of the symbolism, and not take the numbers as literally "so many."

Why Were Symbols Used? This use of symbols confuses us, but symbols had meaning for John's readers. Moreover, they were safe. John, a political exile, was writing about the overthrow of the government to those already suspected of disloyalty. Such a message could be written safely only in symbols.

Principles of Interpretation.[8] Let us state briefly our principles of interpretation.

1. The pictures in the book are symbolic primarily of the events and enemies of John's day, though these events and enemies may be types of like things in all ages.

2. Especially in the prophetic part (chapters 4—22) we must not try to interpret literally, but must seek the truth symbolized by the pictures and numbers used.

3. As is also true in the case of parables like the Prodigal Son, we must not try to find a meaning for every detail of the picture, but seek its main message.

4. Much of the symbolism of the book comes from the Old Testa-

---

[6] For further information see Richardson, pp. 24-33; Love, pp. 42-43.
[7] Matthew 18:21-22.
[8] On principles of interpretation see Hendriksen, chs. I—VI.

ment, so we should see what light is thrown by it on the symbolism in Revelation. However, through old symbolism, *a new message* is given to John, so there will be differences.[9]

III. THE INTRODUCTION AND THE VISION OF CHRIST

Revelation 1

The Introduction. 1:1-8. This is divided into three paragraphs. The first, verses 1-3, tells us that the book is a *revelation* which God gave *by* Jesus Christ through John to his church of things which *it will* experience. Therefore, blessed are those who hear and *keep* the things written. The time is at hand.

The second paragraph, verses 4-7, gives John's salutation from the Triune God, with special emphasis on the work of Christ on earth (witness, death, and resurrection), and his present royal power, "the ruler of the kings of the earth." John praises Christ for what he has done for his people. He has "loosed us from our sins," and "made us to be a kingdom" and "priests." Verse 7 is a vision of Christ coming for judgment.[10]

In the third paragraph, verse 8, God describes himself as the beginner and finisher of history, the Almighty.

The Circumstances of the Vision of Christ. 1:9-11. John tells us that on the island of Patmos,[11] on the Lord's Day,[12] he saw the vision and received the command to write to the Seven Churches of Asia. On a map in your Bible you can locate these churches. If the map showed the Roman highways, you would see that a messenger starting from Ephesus and following the great roads could make a circuit of these churches in the order named, and so return to Ephesus. These seven churches were not the only churches in the province of Asia, but as Sir William Ramsay has suggested, these churches were the logical

---

[9] See Dummelow, p. 1067, sec. 4; Hendriksen, Ch. VI.

[10] See Revelation 14:14 and Daniel 7:13.

[11] For the author and circumstances of writing, see Westminster Bible dictionary, p. 514; Hendriksen, ch. 1; Love, pp. 49-50.

[12] For "the Lord's day" see Westminster Bible dictionary, p. 362, and the commentaries.

centers from which the message of the book would go out to the churches in their neighborhood. Thus these seven churches were "key" churches. But the number "seven" symbolizes the *complete* church (just as the seven Spirits in verse 4 symbolize the Holy Spirit in all his fullness). The order of naming the churches is *geographical.* The idea that these seven churches represent seven periods of church history has been current since about A.D. 1200, but there is nothing in the book to justify such an interpretation.[13] Each church had its own good and bad points, and the message was primarily for them. But since their condition is similar to that in churches today, we may apply Christ's words to our own church where they fit.

The Vision of Christ. 1:12-16. The vision is of a figure walking in the midst of seven candlesticks. The statements about the garment and girdle (vs. 13) suggest one who is of priestly or kingly dignity. Seven statements are then made about the person of Christ, symbolizing, perhaps, the following: white hair, eternality; eyes, omniscience; feet, strength and stability; voice, majesty and power; hand holding the stars, authority over the churches; sword in mouth, the conquering word; and face, deity and radiant purity.[14]

John Comforted and Commanded. 1:17-19. John, overwhelmed with the vision, falls to the earth and is raised up by Jesus, who says, "Fear not."[15] Then from him who is now the Living Lord, who controls even the place of the dead, comes the command to write.

The Explanation of the Candlesticks and the Angels. 1:20. The candlesticks symbolize the churches as "lights" in the world. If their life and witness does not fulfill this purpose they will be removed. (2:5.) Local churches have "faded out." At times the church as an organization has been "blacked out."

The stars are said to be the *angels* of the churches. The interpretation that these are messengers from the churches is not probable, and it is better to take them as symbolizing either the pastors of the churches, or, even better, as symbolizing the church itself in its inner

---

[13] Richardson, p. 61.
[14] Study the references in the margin of the A.S.V., and see what the commentaries say.
[15] Would John think of the incident on the lake (Matt. 14:27)?

character.[16] Christ knows both what the church *does* and what it *is,* and so as Lord of the church is qualified both to praise and to warn.

IV. THE LETTERS TO THE SEVEN CHURCHES

Revelation 2 and 3

The Purpose of These Letters. The churches to whom these letters were written were about to enter a severe period of persecution. As a sign of their loyalty to the Empire, it was demanded of all that they worship before the image of the Emperor. To refuse meant persecution. (13:12-15.) Would they be able to stand it? Would their light be put out? If they were not faithful till death it would not be because of the power of the enemy but because of their own weak spiritual state. So the Living and Reigning Christ calls them to be among the "overcomers" by encouraging them and by pointing out their faults. These seven letters were written to actual churches about conditions in those churches. But the general exhortation at the end of each letter shows that they had a wider mission for the whole church of Christ.

The Form of These Letters. They follow the same general form, which, in its completeness, has seven parts. These may be seen in the letter to Ephesus: (1) The church addressed, "Unto . . . the church of——"; (2) The characterization of Jesus who speaks, "These things saith he——"; (3) Commendation, "I know thy works——"; (4) Criticism, "Nevertheless I have somewhat against thee——"; (5) Warning, "Remember . . . and repent——"; (6) Encouragement, "But this thou hast——"; and (7) A general promise to any who hear, "To him that overcometh——." All seven are found in the letters to Ephesus and Thyatira, but the others lack certain of the seven. Christ has no warning for Smyrna or Philadelphia. He has no commendation for Laodicea, and little for Sardis.[17]

A Method of Study. On a large sheet of paper draw seven columns

---

[16] For a discussion of the meaning of angels, see the Westminster Bible dictionary.
[17] See Love, pp. 57-58.

representing these seven churches. Divide each column into seven parts. In the first of each put the name of the church addressed; in the second, the characterization of Christ who speaks; in the third, the commendation, if any, etc. When filled out for all seven churches you will have material for your study. Ask yourself, Why this particular statement for this church? (You will find that the characterization of Jesus and the promise are often closely related, and both have a definite bearing on the situation in the church.) What does Christ commend in the churches—large membership? Wealth? Buildings? What? What would he commend in our churches today? What does Christ criticize in these churches? What of our churches today? What encouragements and promises are held out for the churches? Which can we appropriate?

Symbolism. There is symbolism to be interpreted in both the characterization of Christ who speaks and in the general promise to the overcomer. Study its meaning. In regard to the promises, you will find many of the same symbols in the Old Testament and in Revelation 21 and 22, and you may readily grasp their meaning. Others are more difficult, but don't be content till you find some satisfactory meaning, and check your findings by the interpretations given in commentaries.

Not Condemnation but Salvation. The two churches in which Christ found no fault have continued till our own day. The others are all gone. Yet, even as God did not send his Son into the world to condemn the world, but to save it (John 3:17), so Jesus did not write these letters as verdicts of condemnation. Even Laodicea, in which he found nothing to commend, was not beyond his saving love. Jesus stood at the door and knocked. Men may be so hardened in their sin that they will not repent, but God in his mercy still seeks their salvation. We may despair of the world and the church, but God in Christ came to save those who were beyond hope. "He that hath an ear, let him hear."

V. THE THRONE, THE BOOK, AND THE LAMB

Revelation 4 and 5

The Purpose of Chapters 4 and 5. Review the structure of the book given in our first study. There it will be seen that the conflict between the forces of good and evil are pictured in chapters 4 to 20, and may be divided into two sections. Chapters 4 through 11 emphasize the controlling hand of God Almighty in the affairs of earth; the judgment of the wicked and the protection of the saints are both from him. Chapters 12 through 20 emphasize the attack and seeming triumph of the forces of evil over the church and then their final overthrow. Chapters 4 and 5 are closely related to the first of these sections, but are also, in a sense, the introductory vision for the whole conflict. Here we are introduced to the real controlling forces in this great conflict, God Almighty and the Lamb, and the conflict is looked at from the point of view of heaven, and things which puzzle men are seen to be from God and under his control.[18]

The Vision of the Throne. 4:1-3. John sees a throne in heaven, but God who sits upon it is beyond his description, and his glorious attributes can only be suggested by symbolic details. We cannot be dogmatic about the meaning of these symbols, and the reader should beware of anyone who is absolutely sure that he can say the final word about them. Consult the commentaries for their suggestions. Perhaps the sardius and the emerald symbolize the judgment and mercy of God, and the thunder and lightning (in vs. 5) the power and glory of God.

The Attendants. 4:4-11. Two groups praise the everlasting God who is worthy to receive glory and honor because he is the creator of all things. The first group, the twenty-four elders, are best taken as symbolizing the redeemed of both the Old Testament and the New Testament times who form one group before God.[19] The other group, the four living creatures are probably the cherubim, the

---

[18] For the central thought of these chapters see Richardson, pp. 76-77; Love, pp. 63-66.

[19] Hendriksen, p. 104; Richardson, p. 69; Westminster Bible dictionary, "Elder," p. 157.

guardians of the throne, although some take them to symbolize the forces of nature subject to God.[20]

The Sealed Book. 5:1-4. There is a sealed book in the hand of God. This book symbolizes God's will in the course and outcome of the conflict between the good and the evil in human history. It is sealed. He who can unseal it will not only reveal to men something of its contents, but must also be able to carry into effect the will of God written there. Who is able to do this?

The Lamb Takes the Book. 5:5-14. The search for one worthy is dramatic suspense from man's side. God knew who would take the book. John hears, "The Lion . . . hath overcome," and he turns and sees "a Lamb standing, as though it had been slain," having seven horns (perfect power) and seven eyes (filled with the Spirit of wisdom). He takes the book (symbolizing his acceptance of the work), and the hosts of heaven—the elders, the living creatures, the angels, and "every created thing"—burst into joyous praise to God Almighty and to the Lamb who is worthy to receive glory and honor. Heaven rejoices because one has been found who can carry out God's will and overcome the forces of evil and establish the good.

The Truth Here Symbolized. Jesus who died for the redemption of the saved (5:9) is now worthy (qualified) to be God's Vice-regent, our Mediatorial King. Read Isaiah 53:12; Philippians 2:9; Matthew 28:18. See what Peter says in Acts 2:33. The crucified Christ has been exalted to the right hand of God and now exercises the power of God for men. This symbolic scene given us in chapter 5 is then the picture of the exalted Christ after his ascension undertaking the work of King. In his hands now rest the destinies of men. He is Saviour and he is Judge.[21]

VI. THE OPENING OF THE SEALS
Revelation 6:1—8:1

How Is the Book Sealed? This question has a bearing on the interpretation of what follows. It has been suggested that the book was

---

[20] Hendriksen, p. 105-107; Love, p. 64; Richardson, p. 70; Westminster Bible dictionary, "Cherub," p. 99.

[21] Hendriksen, pp. 110-111.

sealed in seven parts, the first part being revealed when the first seal was opened, etc. However, the picture suggests that it was completely (seven) sealed, the seals being on the outside in a row.[22] Thus the content of the book could not be read till all the seals were opened. If this was the case (as we think it was), then the opening of the seals would not reveal anything new, but would rather symbolize the elements of the situation, the materials with which God will work. We have pictured here things true in John's day (and also true today) which set forth the means of judgment and also the necessity of judgment.

The Structure of the Section. The seals fall into a group of four (the four horsemen) and three others. Between the sixth and the seventh seals is introduced a parenthetical scene. The seals suggest judgment; the parenthetical section gives us two scenes of those who are safe from judgment.

The First Four Seals. 6:1-8. All agree that the second, third, and fourth seals symbolize war, economic scarcity, and death. Some regard the first, the rider on the white horse, as symbolizing "conquest." But in keeping with Psalm 45:3-6 and Revelation 19:11, it seems better to regard it as symbolizing the progress of the gospel.[23] In the providence of God the conquering gospel goes forth, but the other three also represent agencies "given"[24] by God for functions in the world. Men in John's day experienced them as we do today. For the wicked they are means of judgment and should lead to repentance.[25] For the saved they are means of grace, leading them to realize the sustaining love of God.[26] The gospel is also both a saving and a condemning force. (John 12:44-48; II Cor. 2:14-16.)

The Fifth and Sixth Seals. 6:9-17. Here are given us the moral demand for justice[27] and the wicked's fear of the wrath of God. Conscience in man produces both. Seal six symbolizes man's convic-

---

[22] Hendriksen, pp. 108-109.
[23] Hendriksen, pp. 113-119; Richardson, pp. 79-80; for the opposing view see Love, p. 67.
[24] Note "was given," vss. 2, 4, and 8.
[25] See Section VII on the trumpets.
[26] Romans 8:35-39.
[27] Hendriksen, p. 128; Richardson, pp. 84-85; Love, pp. 69-70.

tion that he merits judgment for sin and his feeling that in earthquakes, etc., he is in the hands of the God of wrath. Thus is pictured a *fear* of the final judgment, but not the judgment itself, for who can flee from the final judgment? (Vss. 15-16.) The cry is, Who can stand in that day? The answer follows.

The Safety of God's People in This Present Age. 7:1-17. This is symbolized by two scenes. The first, the sealing of the 144,000. (7: 1-8.) Here the twelve tribes represent the whole number of God's people on earth. This is the church in conflict. God has numbered his own, and the number is not a small one (12x12x1000). They are safe in the midst of the perils of life. The second scene (7:9-17) pictures for us the church in glory. These are the "overcomers" (vs. 14) who praise God for their salvation (vs. 10).[28]

The Seventh Seal. 8:1. The last element in John's day (and today) is, "The end is not yet." It is not indefinitely postponed—the silence is but for a half-hour. But the final judgment is not yet revealed.[29] And so today. By faith we look for it, and it will come, even though 1900 years have passed since the book was written.

VII. THE FIRST SIX TRUMPETS

Revelation 8:2—9:21

The Trumpet Series as a Whole. Although the final judgment has not come (seventh seal), God does not leave the wicked unwarned and unpunished. In John's day and today in the disasters of nature and in the experiences of men both in their struggle with the forces of evil and with each other, men may see the judgment of God upon their sins. The judgment of the trumpets is partial, not complete and final.[30] Its objective is that men should repent, though it may fail in this objective.[31] The trumpets, like the seals, fall into two groups, a four and a three, with some parenthetical scenes between the sixth and seventh trumpets.

[28] Hendriksen, pp. 132-138; Richardson, p. 88; Love, pp. 70-71.
[29] Compare Hendriksen, p. 141; Richardson, pp. 93-94.
[30] Only one-third destroyed as contrasted with "all" in the vials, ch. 16.
[31] Chapter 9:20-21. Compare Amos 4:6-11 and Pharoah's words, Exodus 9:27.

The Introductory Vision. 8:2-6. In the fifth seal is given the cry of the martyrs for justice, "How long, O Master?" Now John sees these prayers ascending to heaven, and being answered by the symbol of fire poured out upon the earth. We do not need to place this outpouring of judgment in the distant future. Even now God is answering the cry of his saints that wickedness be not allowed to triumph unrebuked.

The First Four Trumpets. 8:7-12. These bring disasters upon the earth, the sea, the rivers and springs, and the heavenly bodies. The student may compare them with the plagues of Egypt. (Exod. 7–10.) However, the language used here in Revelation is full of symbolism and we miss the point when we seek a literal meaning. One-third does not mean exactly one out of three, but a partial destruction. The great mountain and the great star are parts of symbolic pictures.[32] Natural disasters may be recognized as judgments of God. The prophets had always seen in them the hand and the warning of God.[33]

The Fifth and Sixth Trumpets. 8:13—9:21. In 8:13 a flying angel announces three woes upon the inhabitants of the earth, each connected with a trumpet yet to sound. Now judgment will fall directly upon *men,* rather than the physical world. We are to view the fifth and sixth trumpets as symbolizing the *present* experiences of the wicked, which should lead them to repentance, but, we are told, did not. (9:20-21.) These are symbolic pictures whose main point is clear, although we cannot explain all of the details of the pictures nor do we need to do so. The fifth trumpet brings upon men a host of evil beings from the bottomless pit whose king is Apollyon, the Destroyer. (Cf. I Peter 5:8.) The judgment men experience here is the

---

[32] Students will always differ as to what is to be taken symbolically and what literally, but we Westerners are prone to be too literalistic and miss the symbolism that is often there. For example, the natural phenomena of Revelation 6:12-14 and 8:12; how are they to be interpreted? Some say these things will actually happen at Christ's return (of course they haven't yet!). Others point out that such language is used of past events in history, as in Isaiah 13:10 in connection with the conquest of Babylon by the Medes, and in Acts 2:16-21 where Peter says the prophecy of Joel has been fulfilled in the descent of the Spirit. In such cases natural disturbances seem to be used symbolically of God's actions and of spiritual forces.

[33] Joel 1:2-14; Amos 4:6-12; Jonah 1:4; Haggai 1:5-11; etc.

torment of being delivered to the forces of evil for a limited season (5 months).[34] This is not a final torment, but one which the wicked in every age have experienced. The sixth trumpet looses the forces of war upon men, wars which are the results of man's sins. (James 4:1-2.) In their spiritual and social miseries men should repent and turn to God, but the sad fact is that many do not. There can be but one end, surely, to God's forbearance. The seventh trumpet must bring the Last Judgment! (Rom. 2:3-5; Rev. 11:15-18.)

VIII. THE PARENTHETICAL SCENES AND THE SEVENTH TRUMPET

Revelation 10 and 11

The Strong Angel, the Seven Thunders, and the Little Book. Chapter 10. The wicked are unrepentant (9:20-21), and John sees an awe-inspiring angel come from heaven. Surely he comes to pronounce the verdict of God required by the situation. At his voice the seven thunders sound, and John understands their message but is forbidden to reveal it. Some things about the future are not for us to know now. But of one thing the angel assures men; *when* the seventh trumpet sounds there will be no more delay. (Vss. 5-6.) Some other things are to be made known through John (vs. 11), and these are symbolized by the little book, and its message is both sweet and bitter; sweet because it tells of the safety and victory of God's people, bitter because it foretells the suffering through which they must pass.[35] We are given a preview of the contents of the little book in the next two parenthetical scenes (11:1-13) and then a fuller view of it in chapters 12—20.

The Temple Measured and the Two Witnesses. 11:1-13. There is a wide difference in the interpretation of the symbolism of these two scenes due to the difference in the fundamental viewpoint of the various schools of interpreters. The interpretation we give here is in

---

[34] For further suggestions as to the interpretations of these six trumpets, see Hendriksen, pp. 140-148; Richardson, pp. 94-100; Love, pp. 72-75; Dummelow, pp. 1079-1080.

[35] On chapter 10 see Love, pp. 75-78; Hendriksen, pp. 149-151; Richardson, pp. 101-102.

harmony with our belief that in these verses the events on earth between the first and second comings of Christ are pictured for us.

John is told to measure the "temple" (the holy place) with its altar and worshipers, but to leave out the court, which, along with the holy city, is to be trodden by the Gentiles forty-two months. What is symbolized? It is generally agreed that the temple symbolizes God's true people, the church. The court is either a reference to the Jewish synagogue (3:9), or to nominal Christians. The measuring is symbolic of taking under protection. The forty-two months (3½ years) is symbolic of a period of suffering. Here then is the joyful assurance that God's true people will be protected during a period of persecution and suffering.[36]

The two witnesses, however, show that this preservation of the church in this age is not a preservation *from* suffering but *through* suffering. The two witnesses symbolize the church in its missionary work which will continue till its work is accomplished.[37] The beast symbolized the Roman Empire of John's day, and so may symbolize any opposing government. The enemies of the church seem to triumph (vss. 7-10), but God turns that seeming triumph into defeat (vs. 11), even as he did when he raised Christ from the dead. The opposing power will be overthrown (symbolized by the earthquake, vs. 13). The "blood of the martyrs is the seed of the church"; the remnant gave glory to God. (Vs. 13.) So it was with pagan Rome, and so in faith we know it will always be.

The Seventh Trumpet 11:14-19. Again we reach "the end," but the events are only proclaimed, not described. The kingdom of this world has become the Kingdom of our Lord and his Christ.[38] Through the praise of the church we learn that God now acts. The time has come for the dead to be raised and the final judgment to be visited on the good and the wicked. (Vs. 18.) The opened temple, with the ark revealed, has been taken as a symbol of both God's

---

[36] On 11:1-2 see Hendriksen, pp. 152-155; Love, pp. 78-79; Richardson, p. 103; Dummelow, p. 1081.

[37] On the two witnesses, see Hendriksen, pp. 155-159; Love, pp. 79-80; Richardson, pp. 104-105; Dummelow, p. 1081.

[38] See Love, p. 81.

mercy and his judgment, but the thunder and lightnings seem to be more in line with the latter.[39]

IX. THE CHURCH AND HER PERSECUTORS

Revelation 12:1—14:5

Chapters 12 Through 20 Are a Unit. They picture the seeming triumph and final judgment of the enemies of the church. In chapters 4—11 the wicked are helpless but unrepentant under the judgment of God. Only in the "preview" (11:3-13) does the *conflict* between the forces of good and evil come to view. But in chapters 12 —20 this is the chief theme. Chapter 12:1-12 introduces us to the leading antagonists and describes Christ's crucial victory over Satan, the "dragon." The sections that follow picture how the dragon and his two allies turn on the followers of Christ. At first they seem to have the upper hand, but one after the other their final doom is described. For convenience we are dividing these chapters into three studies, although we feel that there are four natural divisions: chapters 12—14; 15—16; 17:1—19:10; and 19:11—20:15.

The Symbolic Characters. Chapters 12—14 introduce us to the radiant woman, her child, and their enemies, the dragon, the two beasts, and the harlot city. All of these are symbolic and their conflict is pictured in symbolic terms. What did they mean for John's readers? We can but sketch the meaning, in this section taking the first six paragraphs. (12:1—14:5.)[40]

The Woman and the Dragon. 12:1-6. The woman is the body of God's people from whom Christ after the flesh was born. The devil, recognizing his enemy, seeks to destroy Christ (at birth, temptation, crucifixion), but the ascension (vs. 5) reveals his defeat. The woman remains on earth, protected like Elijah (I Kings 17:1-7) for 1260 days.[41]

---

[39] See Hendriksen, pp. 159-161; Richardson, pp. 105-107.

[40] For a fuller discussion see Love, pp. 82-93; Hendriksen, pp. 162-185; Richardson, pp. 108-120; Dummelow, pp. 1082-1084.

[41] See Revelation 11:2, "42 months"; 11:3, "one thousand, two hundred and threescore days." On the meaning of this symbolic 3½ year period see the commentaries.

War in Heaven. Verses 7-12. This picture is parallel with the last, emphasizing not the Devil's failure so much as Christ's victory through his triumphant life and death. It is pictured as a spiritual battle in which Satan is robbed of his power.

The same truth is referred to in Christ's "binding the strong man" (Matt. 12:29); and in the statement in Luke 10:18 and in John 16:11. The power of the Devil to ultimately harm God's own or to thwart God's purpose for men has been broken. He may and does persecute the church (12:15-17), but he cannot overthrow it. His time is short, so he rages against the saints. (12:12.)

The Satanic Persecution of the Church. 12:13—13:18. Satan rages against the saints (12:17) through earthly agents which are pictured for us under the form of two wild beasts. The beast from the sea (13:1-10) is the Roman Empire, pictured as a combination of several wild beasts to show its ferocious power.[42] With the Devil's authority (vs. 2) and God's permission (vs. 7) the beast persecutes and kills the saints. This beast may typify any persecuting political power.

The beast from the land (13:11—18), who is also the false prophet (16:13; 19:20), was in John's day the Provincial Council of Asia, which exercised the power of the Empire and made the enforcement of emperor worship one of its chief concerns, with death as the penalty for refusal. The seven churches were in this province of Asia. This beast may well typify all authorities persecuting under the guise of religion.

The Lamb and the 144,000 on Mount Zion. 14:1-5. Who will be able to withstand the dragon and his two allies? The answer is suggested in 13:8, but John wants to make plain the salvation of the persecuted saints. He has not yet pictured the judgment upon these enemies, but he now draws aside, as it were, a curtain, and gives us a foreview of the end. There we see all of those saints who had been sealed on earth (7:3 ff.) safe and rejoicing in heaven. Not one is missing. Thus we anticipate the voice of 14:13, "Blessed are the dead who die in the Lord."

---

[42] The characteristics of the four world powers of Daniel 7 are here combined into one fearful monster.

X. JUDGMENT ANNOUNCED AND POURED OUT

Revelation 14:6—19:10

The Announcement and Pictures of the Harvest-Judgment. 14: 6:20[43] These paragraphs conclude the section, chapters 12—14. Three angelic voices announce that the hour has come, Babylon is fallen, and judgment falls on those having the mark of the beast. (Vss. 7-12.) Then John hears a voice declaring the blessedness of those who died in the Lord. (Vs. 13.) This is followed by two pictures: Christ gathering the saved at God's command (vss. 14-16), and an angel reaping grapes to be cast into the wine press of the wrath of God (vss. 17-20). Thus again we are brought to the final judgment, but in the chapters which follow, John presents successive pictures of the fate that overtakes each of the enemies.

The Seven Last Plagues Poured Out. Chapters 15—16.[44] This series emphasizes judgment (not warning as in the trumpets), and is poured out upon those having the mark of the beast (14:9-11; 16:2) and upon their headquarters, the city "Babylon" (14:8; 16:10, 19). The contents of these "bowls" (sometimes translated "vials") are not to be taken literally; they are symbolic of final and comprehensive judgment on God's enemies. The sixth and seventh bowls are of special interest. The sixth, as in the trumpets, is poured out on the Euphrates, preparing the way for marching armies. The armies of the wicked, incited by the propaganda (frogs) from the mouth of the dragon and his allies, come to wage a "showdown" battle with God Almighty at a place called Har-Magedon or Armageddon.[45] The battle and its outcome will be pictured later in 19:17-21. We would expect the seventh bowl to bring the final end of *all* of God's enemies, but the picturing of the doom of the two beasts (the sea-born beast and the earth-born beast or false prophet) and the dragon is reserved for later treatment. (19:20 and 20:10.) What is said to

---

[43] Hendriksen, pp. 185-188; Richardson, pp. 121-128; Love, pp. 94-96; Dummelow, p. 1084.

[44] Love, pp. 96-100; Hendriksen, pp. 189-198; Richardson, pp. 129-142; Dummelow, pp. 1085-1086.

[45] Hendriksen, pp. 195-197; Richardson, pp. 139-140; Love, pp. 98-99.

be "done" (16:17) here is the overthrow of "Babylon" whose doom was announced in 14:8.[46]

The Magnificence and Judgment of Babylon. Chapters 17—18.[47] John turns a moment to marvel at Babylon and its fall. By "Babylon" is symbolized the great city of Rome, the "harlot" or seducer from God in her age as were Ninevah (Nahum 3:4) and Tyre (Isa. 23 and Ezek. 26:1—29:19) before her. Rome in John's day was the great rival of God, offering to men "the lust of the flesh and the lust of the eyes and the vainglory of life" (I John 2:16), and she is a type of the "world" today which seduces men from God. The pagan Rome that reigned over the kings of the earth (17:18) passed, and so will every godless center of civilization.

In 18:1-8 comes the call to God's people to come out of her that they may not share her doom. Then follows a threefold lament over her by the kings of the earth, the merchants, and the seamen, for the political and economic life is disrupted by her fall. (Vss. 9-19.) But for the saints the fall of "Babylon" brings joy, for thereby is vindicated the righteousness of God. (Rev. 17:6-14; 18:5-8, 20.) The completeness of her fall is symbolized by a millstone cast into the sea. (18:21-24.)

The Heavenly Hallelujahs. 19:1-10[48] The call to joy in 18:20 is now answered by a great multitude in heaven, praising God for his righteousness in overthrowing "Babylon." (19:1-6.) There is also a second cause for joy, for now "the marriage of the Lamb is come," with its accompanying supper. (Vss. 7-10.) Jewish thought had often pictured the joys of the Messianic age under the figure of a feast, and this figure is found in the New Testament in Matthew 8:11; 22:2-14; Luke 14:15-24; etc. God's people had been pictured as given in marriage to God or Christ both in the Old Testament and in the New. John here combines both figures to express the perfect relationship and the joy of the people of God when evil has been overthrown and the new age has come. This bliss is given under another figure in chapters 21 and 22.

---

[46] Love, pp. 99-100.

[47] Hendriksen, pp. 199-213; Richardson, pp. 142-148; Love, pp. 100-104; Dummelow, pp. 1086-1088.

[48] See Hendriksen, pp. 213-217; Richardson, pp. 148-150; Love, pp. 104-106.

XI. THE FINAL VICTORY

Revelation 19:11—20:15

The Structure of This Section. It falls into three main divisions: the overthrow of the beasts and their followers (19:11-21); the overthrow of Satan (20:1-10); and the final judgment of all men (20:11-15). The important questions are: (1) What is the time and character of the conquest of the Word of God? (19:11-21.) (2) Does 20:1-10 follow chapter 19 in time, or is it a parallel to it? (3) When and in what respect is Satan bound, and what is meant by the picture of the saints living and reigning with Christ? (20:1-10.) (4) Who is judged in the final scene? (20:11-15.) Our understanding is that the first two divisions begin with the events of John's day, the first foretelling the overthrow of persecuting Rome, the second picturing the whole church age, ending with the final defeat of Satan. The last scene is the final judgment of all men.

The Word on the White Horse. 19:11-16.[49] All agree that this symbolizes Christ. Some, however, believe that this pictures his Second Coming to judgment, and therefore the "beast" and the "false prophet" who are destroyed are some future manifestations of evil. Others, who feel that in the earlier chapters the beast is clearly the Roman Empire, feel that John is also speaking of the defeat of pagan Rome here. We have previously had pictured judgment upon those who had the mark of the beast (chs. 15—16), and on "Babylon" (chs. 17—18). Now is clearly pictured the final destruction of the beasts (19:20), which has not been described for us before.

The Nature of the Conquest of Christ. 19:17-21. The forces of evil are certainly overthrown and the evil systems are destroyed (the beasts thrown into the lake of fire, vs. 20). The followers were "killed with the sword . . . which . . . came forth out of his mouth" (vs. 21). How does Christ conquer his enemies? On first thought we might say by blotting them out, condemning them to eternal punishment. But this is only a partial answer. We all (and all the multitude of the saved in heaven) were once enemies of Christ.

---

[49] On Revelation 19:11-21 see Love, pp. 106-108; Hendriksen, pp. 217-220; Richardson, pp. 151-156; Dummelow, pp. 1088-1089.

(Rom. 5:10.) Christ conquered us and we became his slaves and loyal followers. To put down evil does not necessarily mean to crush evil by final punishment. The enemies may be transformed into friends. Persecuting Rome was destroyed, but the city of Rome was not. The kingdom of this world may be hostile to Christ, but it will become the Kingdom of Christ, and the kings of the earth shall bring their glory and honor into the New Jerusalem. (Rev. 11:15; 21:24.) We are told here that his victory comes through the sword of his mouth. (19:21.) Surely this is not a steel blade but the spoken word. That spoken word may condemn (Matt. 25:41; John 12:46-48), but Jesus' great purpose was not condemnation but salvation (John 3: 16-19; 12:47), and by the word which may condemn, others are born into the Kingdom (James 1:18; I Peter 1:23). It is a fact of history that persecuting Rome was overthrown by the gospel of Christ.

The Overthrow of Satan. 20:1-10.[50] The overthrow of the hostile Roman Empire and the Emperor worship will be an empty victory unless the dragon who is the real source of the opposition is overthrown. So 20:1-10 turns the spotlight on Satan. In 12:7-12 we were given a picture of a decisive defeat of Satan, and verses 13-17 of that chapter showed that he could not overcome the church, though he might persecute Christians. But even then he could not ultimately harm those he persecuted. In 14:1-5 all the "sealed" (7:4-8) are shown safe in glory. The dead who die in the Lord are blessed. (14: 13.) These same truths are pictured in chapter 20, which goes beyond them, however, to tell us of Satan's final defeat. In 20:1-3 we are told that Satan is bound so that he cannot deceive the nations. His defeat was in the cross of Christ.[51] He cannot triumph over the church. This was made evident in the failure of his agent, the persecuting Roman Empire. However, at the end of this age "he must be loosed" for a little while. (20:3, 7-9.) This is God's *must,* and why it should be is beyond our understanding.

It would seem, though, that at the end of this age there will be a short time when a sudden and widespread apostasy from God will

---

[50] On this much debated section see Hendriksen, pp. 221-235; Richardson, pp. 156-176; Love, pp. 108-118; Dummelow, p. 1089.
[51] See our comments on Revelation 12.

culminate in a final "showdown" between the forces of good and evil. (20:7-9.) The victory over the beasts of John's day (19:20) is a type of the final victory. Gog and Magog symbolize this new and final manifestation of the anti-Christian forces among men. But this revolt is futile, and the forces of evil are destroyed by fire from heaven (vs. 9)[52] and Satan is finally put where he can stir up no more trouble (vss. 9-10).

While Satan is bound for 1,000 years the saints reign. (Vs. 4.) Who reigns? A literal interpretation would require the reigning to be limited to those whom John sees, the martyrs and confessors of the day of the beast, the Roman Empire.[53] Literal interpretation cannot make it apply to *all* the Old and New Testament saints. But symbolically, this limited group may be taken to represent all who have been faithful unto death. The first resurrection has also been interpreted literally. This may be done with consistency if this resurrection is limited to the special groups described in verse 4. But to take it as a *literal* resurrection of those who may be represented *symbolically* by these special groups (i.e., a literal resurrection of all of God's people) is not sane interpretation, but a reading in of the ideas you desire. If the groups in verse 4 are symbolic of all of God's people who overcome, then it would seem to follow that we must take the first resurrection as symbolic of some truth about the "overcomers," and resurrection suggests newness of life. Such symbolism would be fitting here. Verses 4-6 would be another scene (like 7:4-17; 11:11-12; 14:1-5, 13) symbolizing the safety and blessedness of those who "overcome."[54] Being a symbolic vision, all of its details cannot be rationally harmonized any more than can be done with the picture of Christ (1:14-16), or the woman, dragon, and child (12:1-5). Perhaps these truths would be symbolized: Those who overcome will enter into an "abundant life," they "reign." (John 10:10; Rom. 5:17; Rev. 22:5; etc.) They are in immediate fellowship with God in

---

[52] This fire from God may well symbolize Christ's Second Coming. Compare II Thessalonians 1:7-10.

[53] Those who put this section of the book into the future and consider the beast to be the future Antichrist, would have to limit these groups to the martyrs and confessors of the time of the Antichrist.

[54] Study the promises to "the overcomers" given in chapters 2 and 3.

Christ, "reign with him," are "priests of God." They are eternally safe, the "second death" cannot hurt them. Yet their experience is not the final and eternal state of bliss. This is for a thousand years; [55] the final state knows no end. (Rev. 22:5.) The church has always believed that no matter how blessed may be the dead in Christ *now*, nevertheless after they have been clothed in their resurrection bodies, they will experience an increase of blessedness.

The Judgment of the Great White Throne. 20:11-15.[56] All stand before the throne, the small and the great, and all not found written in the book of life are cast into the lake of fire, for by the record of men's "works" (the "books" of vs. 12), all men stand condemned, for all have fallen short of the glory of God (Rom. 3:23). The resurrection has overcome death, and Hades (the land of departed spirits) is now empty, so their end is symbolized by their being cast into the lake of fire. The church through the ages has always seen in this picture the final judgment of *all men*. The idea that it is the final judgment of the *wicked only* originated among the Plymouth Brethren about a century ago.

XII. THE ETERNAL BLESSEDNESS OF GOD'S PEOPLE. THE EPILOGUE

Revelation 21 and 22

The Structure. With chapter 20 the conflict is over. The good and evil have been permanently separated, and we now have symbolized in 21:1—22:5 the blessed life of the saved. In 21:1-8 the emphasis is on the symbol of a "new earth" (with its city). In 21:9—22:5 the symbol of the New Jerusalem is developed. In 22:6-21 we have the closing words of the book.[57]

The New Earth. 21:1-8. The emphasis is upon "new" (four times). Again we must look for truth in symbolism; "the sea is no more" makes that evident. The truth symbolized is that then God's people will live in an earth "wherein dwelleth righteousness." (II

---

[55] A thousand years symbolizes a long but not endless period of time (10x10x10).
[56] See Hendriksen, pp. 235-236; Richardson, pp. 176-181; Love, p. 118.
[57] Love, pp. 125-128; Hendriksen, pp. 236-256; Richardson, pp. 181-195; Dummelow, pp. 1090-1092.

Peter 3:13.) Now we live in a world of mixed good and evil. Then all the evil will be in the lake of fire. (19:20; 20:10, 15.) In the new earth is the New Jerusalem, the ideal dwelling place of God's children, where they will live with him, free from the pains and sorrows of this life. Study the symbolism.

The New Jerusalem. 21:9—22:5. What is symbolized here? The New Jerusalem is said to be "the bride, the wife of the Lamb." (21:9.) Here is familiar symbolism. In the Old Testament (e.g., Isa. 54:5) God's people are often spoken of as God's wife (though they are often unfaithful to him!). In the New Testament (e.g., Eph. 5: 25-27) the church is pictured as the bride of Christ, so this title in Revelation 21:9 unites the two, making the New Jerusalem symbolic of all of God's people, loved by him, and made glorious, "not having spot or wrinkle or any such thing." (Eph. 5:27.)

But the New Jerusalem is also described as a city (21:10) which has foundations (Heb. 11:10). Its various parts are measured and described. But we will go off on the wrong track if we think these things give us a literal description of heaven. Have we forgotten that the New Jerusalem is a bride? Christ does not marry streets of gold and precious stones, but is united to a people. So the city is a symbol of God's people, and all of the descriptions are to symbolize truths about their blessedness.

We may differ as to the interpretation of some of these symbols, but we must agree that it is the beauty and perfections of the life of God's people that are symbolized. Study the symbolism. What does city suggest—safety? permanence? rich, co-operative life? Perhaps all of these. What do the walls and gates and streets of gold, etc., suggest? It will be of interest to search through these chapters and list what is said to be absent (no sea, tears, death, etc.), and then to see what positive statements are made (ever-open gates, 21:25; river, 22:1; tree of life, 22:2; etc.). What do all these symbolize? One of the great emphases is the dwelling of God in unbroken and unbarred fellowship with his people. An old promise (Exod. 6:7 and on through the Old Testament) is now fulfilled (Rev. 21:3). The Temple was both a meeting place and a hiding place for God. In the New Jerusalem there is no temple, but in unbroken and unclouded light, his people dwell in God's presence. (21:22-23.) In connection with these chapters it is worth while to re-read the whole book, noting especially what is promised to God's people in chapters 2 and 3, and what is said about their blessedness in the various visions (5: 9-10; 7:13-17; 15:2-4, etc.).

God Almighty reigneth, and he will continue to reign unopposed. "His servants shall serve him" (22:3), men are obedient to his will, life for the saved will be full and satisfying and varied, each contributing his share (21:24). All are Christlike and live in God's immediate presence. (22:4.) Do we say serve him? Yes, but such will be the quality of life that they are said to "reign for ever and ever." (22:5.)

The Epilogue. 22:6-21. Here we find various ones speaking. The angel affirms the truth and value of the revelation. (Vss. 6-7.) John falls in worship before the angel and is reproved. (Vss. 8-9.) He is told not to seal the book, for the time is at hand—its message was for John's readers, not for a distant age. (Vss. 10-11.) Then Jesus speaks (vss. 12-16); and the Spirit invites (vs. 17); and John warns against tampering with the message of the book and prays for its speedy fulfillment, then closes with the benediction (vss. 18-21).